ACHIEVING CHANGE

A Practical Guide for Creating Online Courses for Workplace Learning

---

HENRIK J. MONDRUP

ISBNs

Paperback: 978-1-989059-58-6

eBook: 978-1-989059-57-9

Audiobook: 978-1-989059-59-3

Learn more: henrikjm.com

Illustrations by

FRANK HØEDT

Praise for HENRIK J. MONDRUP

Henrik will gently guide you away from common pitfalls in learning experience design and put you on an easy-to-follow path to giving your people superpowers.

Emilie White, CEO, Paper Planes

A compelling learner-centered approach to building effective and well-crafted online courses that incorporates how the brain learns with research-driven instructions on how to engage your learners.

Monica Diaz, course operations specialist at Stanford University

In a time where e-learning rightfully is being dismissed for its inability to deliver results, learning professionals need a new digital modus operandi. *Achieving Change* thankfully delivers a well-argued pragmatic approach, enabling you to cause actual change.

Kristoffer Lolk Fjeldsted, digital learning lead, LEO Pharma

Henrik is at the forefront of a new wave of practitioners, exploring how to create impactful learning for a new generation in the workplace. This book is a must-read for faculty, HR, and the learning industry as a whole.

Carl Dawson, co-founder of Construct

Achieving Change is a useful and inspirational book for those who work in the educational sector producing online courses. It presents ways in which acquired knowledge can be transformed into skills, ie the ability to apply knowledge to a practical business situation and further develop it (competences), through online teaching methods.

Keld Hvam, director of e-learning and e-didactics, International Business Academy

A welcome and much needed guide for the busy practitioner designing for online learning. It brings together thoughts on learning, design, engagement and assessment into an easily applicable five step model, which usefulness is explored and exemplified through multiple real-world cases. A great companion for the corporate learning designer.

Thomas Ryberg, professor of digital learning, Aalborg University, Denmark

A cool guide to help L&D professionals create online learning for adults–motivating online learning, that is! In five easy applicable steps he guides you through the entire process ensuring that necessary reflection takes place along the way and that common pitfalls are avoided.

Maiken Lykkegaard, director of education, Danish State Railways (DSB)

An action-oriented guide to developing online courses. With a handful of good examples and – on the surface – a simple model he shows that it is not rocket science to create and deliver powerful learning through online courses.

Per Andersen, vice dean for education, Aarhus BSS, Aarhus University, Denmark

A thoughtful, common sense guide to online learning. It's cleverly presented in a way that's accessible for beginners, yet still thought provoking for people who have been working in this field for years. Mondrup takes us beyond models, research and theory, to see the practicalities of digital learning in the real world.

Matthew Smith, CEO, Purelearning, Australia

An inspiring read for anyone aspiring to provide impactful learning experiences online. Founded on a compelling combination of educational science and common sense, Mondrup offers workable instructions for overcoming some common pitfalls in online learning.

Nicoline Hultén, manager organizational development, people & organizational performance, Lundbeck

Achieving Change serves as a guide steeped in classic instructional principles as well as modern learning science. It's a set of critical and much-needed tools for the modern workplace. Learning design practitioners and subject matter experts alike will undoubtedly keep coming back for Henrik's personal stories and concrete business examples.

Ben Piscopo, senior learning designer, edX.org by Harvard University and MIT

A must read for learning professionals. This amazing book is a practical guide for designing impactful learning. Based on scientific research, best practice and real-life cases, Mondrup demonstrates how his five-step model has proven it's worth helping companies achieving great results through well-designed learning experiences.

Pernille Nielsen, learning program manager, Siemens Gamesa

At last a book that focuses on the practical application of learning theory. Mondrup takes us by the hand and guides us step by step through the minefield that designing and developing learning programmes can be. This is a brilliant, short and to-the-point handbook for good, state-of-the-art learning design that will have a lasting effect on the organisation.

Merete Sievers, Training Partner

Mondrup provides both experienced and less experienced learning professionals with a practical guide for creating engaging and impactful learning. The combination of brain- and learning research with practical, easily applicable instructions on how to design online learning is the unique selling-point of this well-written book.

Cecilie Rosengreen Kringel, senior consultant, leadership & talent, Nykredit

Mondrup challenges the common belief that online learning can only reach knowledge level. Here we go all the way to enhanced competency and thus real change in behaviour which learning is all about!

Mia Louise Rydahl Due, online learning consultant, BoConcept

Henrik Mondrup succeeds in delivering a straightforward model that anyone can use as an excellent starting point for any learning need. The model will challenge most learning professionals to move away from the traditional "information dump" approach and spend more time creating effective solutions. Regardless of whether you are new to the world of digital learning or an experienced practitioner, Achieving Change will be a great asset for you.

Niels H. Rasmussen, learning & development manager, Pandora

People are not what they do for a living, but how they respond to others.

Contents

Section III: Apply

Introduction

I envision a world where people have access to education that allows them to improve their lives. My mission is to help the modern-day educator like you to create effective online learning courses for adults in the workplace.

To help you understand my vision, I'm going to take you back in time and tell you a story about my great-great grandfather. His name was Niels, and he lived on a farm in Denmark in the nineteenth century. Niels, himself the son of a farmer, grew up in an agricultural economy where the majority of the workforce was growing crops. Niels and all his brothers became farmers, educated since childhood in the art of farming. They received information from their dad, watched what he was doing, asked him questions, and imitated his work.

When Niels grew older, he had children himself. However, by the time his children became adults, the world had changed. The economy was transitioning from farming to industrialisation. Sons of farmers, like my great-great grandfather, no longer stayed to take over the farm, instead moving to the city to work in factories. Learning how to do their factory jobs, including working with machines, wasn't that different from how their ancestors had learned on the farms. It was still based on information, observation, and practice.

As industrialisation advanced, the number of companies grew, and new types of jobs emerged. Not only in small Denmark but worldwide. These companies needed qualified leaders, specialists, financiers, and managers. However, there was a mismatch between the number of open positions and the number of qualified people able to fill these jobs. Educational institutions like Harvard Business School (launched 1908) and degree programmes like the Master of Business Administration (MBA) first saw light in large part to address this problem.

Back in the early 1900s, attending university was a privilege reserved for the wealthy, those who grew up in nice homes with good conditions and who, from childhood, learned to develop self-discipline and a motivation to learn. These attributes were important because they were required by universities and teaching institutions whose education method relied on lectures.

Compared to how farmers and industrial workers learned their roles, these university lectures only *passed on* information through a lecture format. They didn't include observation of real-life examples or provide opportunities to practice. For the highly self-disciplined and motivated student, this wasn't a big problem, as they had been conditioned to learn this way.

In the mid-twentieth century, Western society changed again, and industrialism began to give way to the knowledge economy. The majority of the workforce shifted from factory work to the service sector and immaterial production, where knowledge is the most important resource.

During this shift from the industrial to the knowledge economy, my own grandfather was following in his father's footsteps and farming our family's soil. He had three children: my dad, my uncle, and my aunt. My dad followed tradition and is farming on our family's land today. My eldest brother is going to take over after him. However, my dad's siblings became typical workers in the knowledge economy. My aunt became a kindergarten teacher; my uncle an engineer.

In order for my aunt and uncle to produce value in the knowledge economy, through the new commodities of services and immaterial goods, they needed education. But how do you educate a workforce with people from all different backgrounds who have not been raised with the high self-discipline and motivation required to learn in a lecture format? How do you educate students who have different learning preferences, many of whom struggle when their only option is through lectures?

My answer is that you look back to the good old ways of teaching that worked for thousands of years, that worked when my great-great grandfather learned how to farm. Through information, observation, and practical application. And then you implement this teaching approach in the workplace as well as in educational institutions and universities.

This transition to including the centuries-old method of teaching at institutions and universities has actually happened, at least in part. In the 1960s, Harvard University developed problem-based learning as a way to address the learning preferences of learners from different backgrounds compared to traditional university students. Problem-based learning is being used in higher education worldwide today. Today, many certificate and degree programmes—in higher as well as lower education—include mandatory internships where students learn by working with real-world problems. To meet the demands of society you need to meet the demands of each learner. That means delivering learning programmes that reflect *how* they learn.

The knowledge economy is influenced by technology, which constantly changes the skills needed for the workforce. The days where companies could rely on new graduates or other new entrants to the labour market as the main influx of new knowledge and skills are gone. Instead, companies need a workforce that continuously acquires new skills or enhances existing ones. Employees must learn continuously over the course of their careers. As employers, leaders, HR professionals, and educators we need to deliver efficient and flexible learning opportunities. We need to offer education so that the workers can access, absorb, reflect on, and incorporate new knowledge—ideally on their own schedule.

Many corporate leaders saw e-learning as the answer to this growing need for continuous education and have influenced e-learning today. Unfortunately, many of those same leaders possessed the ingrained self-discipline and motivation to learn and were acclimatised to learn through instruction. They don't need to observe, discuss, or practice, and as such they don't think anyone else might need to either. So, the concept of e-learning was created by combining new technology with a century-old way of teaching, which only works for the few. The financiers of the development of e-learning mirrored their own experiences and took care of their own needs, but forgot to consider how the end user learns.

It's not hard to understand why so many employees today hate e-learning. Nor why the completion rate is as low as 5 per cent. These e-learning programmes are not designed for the learning preferences of the majority of the audience and they don't consider their prerequisites to learning. The consequence is that many simply don't learn from these programmes and find them a waste of time.

This is wasteful for the company and frustrating for the learner. I aim to change that.

My purpose in writing this book is to help you create e-learning, online courses, online learning, or whatever you choose to call it, to meet the demands of the majority of learners and their preferred way of learning. I will show you how to combine technology with teaching methods that will enable your employees or students to really learn.

I will show you how to create workplace training that makes a real difference, that generates competitive gains both for the company and the worker. You'll know how to create online courses that result in employees working in new ways or enhancing existing ways of working. I'm talking about achieving meaningful, long-lasting, on-the-job change.

It is possible. I've done it myself.

A Real Life Fairstart

The hour was late. The pressure was high. In Denmark in 1981, Niels Peter Rygaard was struggling to become a psychologist, with a dream to help children at risk. He had been sitting in his room for almost a week trying to finish his master's thesis. Early Sunday morning, his typewriter ran out of ink. With all shops closed his only choice was to pick up a pen and finish by hand. Working all day and all night he managed to finish his thesis, and, with a very sore hand, he handed it to his professor on Monday morning, just in time to meet his deadline.

Shortly after Rygaard graduated with his psychology degree, he started working at a treatment centre for children. After ten years he was teaching treatment and prevention nationwide. His Danish career was flourishing.

However, Rygaard wasn't satisfied. His big dream was to help children around the globe. In 2005 he wrote and published a book, *Severe Attachment Disorder*, a practical guide that shares his experience and methods. The book was well received, translated and published in a number of languages. It led to an international career teaching at universities, special school units, and orphanages around the world. And he created his own company: the Fairstart Foundation.

Even though Rygaard was finally making a difference for children within and beyond the borders of Denmark, he still didn't feel he was fulfilling his dream. He was physically limited by time and logistics and couldn't teach as many people in as many locations as he wanted. He considered and then dismissed e-learning, believing that it would not work well with his teaching method, which required sharing knowledge as well as facilitating a process that would lead to behavioural change.

The solution appeared one day as Rygaard was sitting at his desk, looking through some papers. A description for an upcoming event at the Rotary International Club, a business network he was member of, jumped off the page demanding his attention. The speaker would be talking about "the future of learning." Without hesitation, and without fully understanding why, Rygaard signed up for the event.

He attended the Rotary International event with low expectations. But when he heard the young speaker, he was stunned. In front of the room was a young man saying that technology had finally caught up with proper teaching methods. What's more, this young man knew how to bring them together to create online learning that could facilitate behavioural change. Just what Rygaard needed to fulfill his dream.

Immediately after the lecture, Rygaard approached the speaker and invited him for coffee. Six months later, the speaker and Fairstart announced a complete online training programme that would deliver training to caregivers at orphanages around the world. This training programme would do more than enrich their knowledge, it would also change their on-the-job behaviour.

As you might have guessed, the young speaker at the event was me. And since I helped Rygaard to create his online training programme, life has improved for more than 30,000 orphaned children in more than twenty-eight countries. And that number is still growing. All thanks to technologically-delivered, learning-style-appropriate online education of the caregivers. The online learning outcomes were better than expected. Impartial third-party researchers have tested and confirmed that the children in the care of educated caregivers were doing 20 per cent better than those with caregivers who had not received the online learning.

How did Fairstart's online learning programme achieve such

change? Through understanding the caregivers' preferred way of learning, incorporating instruction, observation and practice—in short, by using the *Achieving Change* approach.

Achieving Change

I developed the *Achieving Change* approach through intense research of learning theory, pedagogy, and science about how the brain works, and through practical, hands-on experience working with clients in international and domestic organisations. I've spent countless long days and nights reading through old dusty books about learning theories dating as far as back as Aristotle as well as hundreds of current cutting-edge research papers. I wanted to know how people learn and how what we know about teaching and learning has developed throughout history.

I drew connections between all the learning theories and designed a simple yet comprehensive five-step process for creating effective online learning programmes. These five steps can be used by any learning designer, workplace educator, or practitioner without the need for an academic background or previous understanding of learning theory. Ultimately, this work will help you create powerful courses that will, in turn, create a long-lasting learning outcome and achieve powerful and positive change.

Book Structure and How to Navigate It

Achieving Change is intended to be read initially from front to back, and then to be referred to as needed.

Section I: Understand

Section one will dig into what online learning is, where it is rooted in history, and why you need online learning to approach Millennials or the later demographic cohorts in your workplace.

Section II: Create

Section two is the core of the book and packed with the five steps you'll follow to create your own online learning course. Each chapter within this section is its own step, starting with Know the Learning Brain. We then move right into Initiate Course Development, Engage the Learner, Create the Scripts, and Assessment for Learning.

Each of the five steps incorporates a segment of the learning experience and a call to action.

1. *Know the Learning Brain.* The first step is to understand the fundamentals of how people learn. I'll share concepts extracted from the most significant learning theories.

2. *Initiate Course Development.* Gain insight into setting learning goals, defining what content you can create to achieve those goals, which tools can support the content, and then how to put it all together. Collectively, we call this "learning design," and you are the "learning designer."

3. *Engage the Learner.* Learn about principles of instructional design for creating engaging content, and then learn how to apply the principles using tools such as problem-centred learning, case studies, storytelling, and interviews.

4. *Create the Scripts.* Here you will learn about Aristotle's three modes of persuasion as well as principles of communicating via video. Then, apply that knowledge in the creation of instructional video, since that's the learning designer's primary tool.

5. *Assessment for Learning.* Assessment itself can be a learning opportunity—in addition to merely measuring learning. We'll talk about various types of assessments, the importance of reflection, how best to give feedback,

and how to measure actual learning and not just participation.

SECTION III: APPLY

Section III is where you'll find detailed case studies with examples of real-life online learning initiatives I've implemented with clients, including the Fairstart Foundation, BESTSELLER, Danish international pharmaceutical company Lundbeck, Henley Business School, Aarhus University in Denmark, and Bimco, the world's largest international shipping association. You'll get the context and have the opportunity to further reinforce what you've learned in Section II.

It's my sincere wish that you enjoy my book, and that when you finish reading it, you set it down with confidence, excited to jump into your own online learning design work.

Section I: Understand

ONE

Challenges of E-Learning

<blockquote>
We agree that first generation online learning was pretty awful. But the world of online training has evolved so much. At the risk of using hyperbole—it's not awful, it's wonderful.

Michael DiPietro, Chief Marketing Officer, ExtensionEngine
</blockquote>

W hether you work in a profit or non-profit organisation, you know it's important to offer your people effective learning opportunities. Easier said than done, until now.

Perhaps you are a learning designer responsible for creating internal training. Perhaps you handle leadership training, sales training, or any other type of training for leadership and management. Or perhaps you're a higher-level university, college, or other education course developer.

You may be a subject matter expert (SME) with a desire to create or improve an online course. You may want to increase the volume

3

and quality of learning opportunities you offer your employees, or it could be that your organisation sells or delivers on-site competence development courses and you want to take those to an online environment.

Maybe you know a little bit about on-the-job training, and you know there must be a better way to get measurable results that you can take to your boss and to the bank. You could be a middle-management decision-maker responsible for learning design and delivery, or a senior executive with responsibility for learning and development.

You may have been struggling with ways to modernise the way you are creating and delivering online learning, and you want to know more about massive open online courses (MOOCs) and how you can use them in a corporate setting.

You may need to convince your employer about the merits of achieving change through online learning. They may express doubts or question whether the cost of online learning development will generate a meaningful return on investment. Getting leadership on board is essential. When creating and implementing a learning programme in the workplace, success is directly proportional to the degree of management connection to—and involvement in—implementation of learning on the job.

Research shows that:

- Without leadership sanction or involvement, only 20 per cent of learning gets implemented on the job.
- When leadership provides learners with time and resources, 66 per cent of the learning gets taken back to the job.
- When leadership and management is engaged and involved, that number jumps to 90 per cent[1].

Implementation of Learning on the job

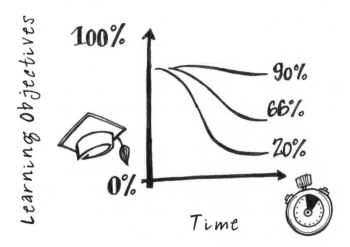

By far the biggest learning event is when an employee first starts a new job. This learning happens through formal, informal, apprenticeship, or other types of on-the-job training.

Advancing technology has increased demands for many of the skills required in most jobs in the knowledge economy. Over and above the skills an employee needs in the direct performance of their role, they also need other, more broadly-applicable skills just to stay competitive in their current role, and yet others if they have any hope of advancing. There is also a premium placed on flexibility.

Computers, smartphones, tablets, watches, and so on, are changing workplaces rapidly, for better or for worse. If your organisation is to attract and keep top talent, you *must* use proper training and learning methods to keep them interested, motivated, and growing—and properly trained.

Common Pitfalls of Online Learning

Perhaps you're in the middle of the learning design or development process but you keep bumping into roadblocks. Or maybe you've already delivered a course but didn't get the results you were hoping for. Here are some of the common pitfalls that you may recognise:

- THE COURSE IS BEING CREATED BY A SUBJECT MATTER EXPERT (SME), BUT THEY AREN'T A TRAINING EXPERT. It takes more than subject matter expertise to create and deliver a training programme or course that changes the way the learner behaves on the job. If you are an SME expert but not an expert in online learning design, not to worry, just apply your ability to the five steps I've laid out and learning is inevitable.

- I JUST WASTED MY TIME AND MONEY ON A BAD COURSE. A good course engages the learner and ensures that what they learn will stick and that they'll apply it. You will discover many techniques to ensure positive results that will bring you a good return on your investment.

- I DELIVERED A COURSE THAT 'WENT SOUTH' AND NOW MY CREDIBILITY IS DAMAGED. A poorly designed and developed online-learning offering will affect reputations: yours, that of your learning department, and perhaps your entire company. If your company creates ten courses and just one of them is of bad quality, you can easily lose credibility. That's enough to potentially put the learner off from taking part in the other nine. *Achieving Change* will give you the framework you need to create high quality courses every time.

Consider your own organisation, its learning programmes, and your challenge in redesigning them to achieve real change. I'll wager one or more of the following problems sounds familiar:

- I want to create online courses, but I don't know how or where to start.
- I don't know how to design learning that leads to change.
- I have no idea how to make learning engaging.
- Is what I'm doing now the right thing? I think I need tools and a helping hand to lead me through the journey step by step.
- I understand the importance of combining formal learning with on-the-job training, but I don't know the best way to do it.
- I've created offline courses, and I know that offline and online training methods are NOT interchangeable, but I don't know how to convert my traditional material into workable online material.
- What is social learning? If I don't understand exactly what it is, I most certainly can't create it.

You're in good company. In *Achieving Change*, I will help you solve all of these problems, and more.

TWO

Putting the Digital in Learning

    Now institutions must begin preparing their system for the digital movement.

George Siemens, co-inventor of MOOCs

M y father is a traditional Danish man. He is hard-working, structured, and a bit skeptical when it comes to trying something new. One day, he and I met at a market in Aarhus, a city close to the farm where I was raised.

"Look son, there's a coffee stall. Can I buy you a coffee?" he asked.

"No thank you, but you go ahead. I'm going to look at these," I pointed to a delicious looking display of pastries.

"Okay," he smiled and strolled over to the coffee stall, digging into his pockets for money. I quickly lost myself in the smells of the fresh baking when about two minutes later my father returned—empty handed.

"Father, where is your coffee?" I asked.

"I tried to pay with cash, but they only accept mobile payment, and I just recently learned how to use a credit card!" he explained.

My father was unable to get his coffee because he hadn't yet adapted to modern technology. It was such a simple thing, a coffee, yet without a working understanding of how to use relatively recent technology, he didn't get his treat.

Just like my father, organisations also need to adapt to technology if they are to get what they want. To get the most out of that technology, they also need to have a firm grip on the underlying ideas upon which it rests. Technology is driven by information and information is driven by technology, so everyone in knowledge-based workplaces needs to continuously learn—and do things in new ways—to keep up with our evolving culture.

There is a Danish proverb that says, "A dear child has many names." The "dear child" in this case is learning. The child has been called classroom training, textbook, workshop, corporate retreat, then e-learning, and now online learning. Our dear child is growing like a weed! She is different from the traditional e-learning of the past yet is born out of technological advancements in e-learning software. I will often use the term 'digital learning' because it encompasses all that you'll find in e-learning, online learning, and mobile learning. But it is all still learning.

Let me unpack the term "digital learning." Like the terms "e-learning," "online learning," or "mobile learning," digital learning is an umbrella term that encompasses educational programmes, courses, or offerings facilitated by technology, where each learner exercises some degree of control over time, place, path and/or pace of learning. Predominantly, online learning requires you to be online. Mobile learning is only for mobile devices. I often use the term digital learning, because it encompasses all that you'll find in e-learning, online learning, or even mobile learning.

Fad or Future?

During my Bachelor of Science studies, where I majored in educational science (a mix of psychology, sociology, philosophy, and pedagogy) I discovered Udacity, one of the pioneers in massive open online courses (MOOCs) that you'll read more about in Chapter 3: A Model History. I got so excited about the potential of online education that I wrote my bachelor thesis on Udacity. And then I obtained a master's degree in Information Technology & Learning.

During my master's I started speaking in front of small business networks about online learning, which even then I believed was the future of education, and I met a lot of skepticism. After one presentation, a respected and influential man stood up in front of an audience and told me that I was never going to succeed, and that online learning was just a passing fad. My stomach and my throat changed places that day. For a while, I wondered if maybe he was right, and I was wrong. But I didn't quit. Instead, I decided to focus on how to overcome the challenges his viewpoint presented. I knew he was wrong, and I wanted to prove it.

Six short years after that experience, more than 100,000,000 people worldwide had enrolled in online courses. Quite the fad. Meanwhile, my career in online learning has rocketed right along with the popularity of online learning. It's not a fad. It's here to stay and grow. Organisations must adapt and master.

After my first presentation to a local Rotary club in Aarhus, Rotary members around Denmark began contacting me, wanting to know more, and wanting to work with me. Soon, Hans Middleburg, my former mentor, offered to act as a business advisor, and he invited me to a dinner where I met international politicians including the Dutch and Chinese ambassadors to Denmark. Since then, I've given many, many presentations to companies and universities in Denmark, Europe, as well as the USA. I was delighted, for instance, when edX invited me to speak at the May 2017 Open edX conference in Spain, organised by Harvard and

MIT. I'm proud of my work and excited about the interest others show in it.

What Needs to Change

One of the most common teaching methods I often meet and fight against is the old petrol-pump approach is where teachers think it's enough to squeeze the nozzle, release a flow of information expecting that this fills the students' heads with knowledge, and call it a day. Many educators are still using that approach, and it's bleeding into corporate learning. However, this long-standing tradition is now challenged by a generation wanting flexible and just-in-time learning that leads to tangible results. We have a disconnect.

- Employees who are inadequately trained experience more work-related stress and are less likely to perform.
- Ninety-three per cent of Millennials consider ongoing skills development as key to their careers and want access

to lifelong learning opportunities and are willing to spend their own resources on training.[1]

- Seventy-one per cent of those likely to leave their organisations in the next two years are similarly dissatisfied with how their leadership skills are being developed.[2]

Despite the disconnect, many institutions, corporations, and other workplaces still operate on the assumption that learning is a competition of filling as much knowledge as possible into the learner's head, in as short amount of time as possible.[3] When it comes time to assess whether learning has, in fact, occurred, we ask the learner to demonstrate their new knowledge, often outside any work-related context, by demonstrating they can remember facts and numbers. This is known as 'teaching for the test'. It's no wonder that many learners consider institutional education irrelevant: the learning that does take place is boring and tedious and/or that learning is not for them.

Research has confirmed that distance/online learning—if designed the right way—is at least as effective, if not more effective, as traditional classroom-style instruction.[4]

A study from Harvard and MIT revealed just how effective and important online learning can be:

- Of 27,000 respondents, 87 per cent reported career benefits from participating in an online course
- Thirty-three per cent reported tangible career benefits (pay raise, promotion, new job)
- Of 14,000 respondents, 88 per cent reported educational benefits from participating in an online course
- Eighteen per cent reported tangible educational benefits (gaining credit toward an academic programme or completing prerequisites for an academic programme)

Universities like Harvard, Stanford, and Oxford, and global companies such as Microsoft, Deloitte, and Facebook are launching online learning in their academic and corporate education programmes.

These elite universities and large organisations no longer debate whether online learning is as good as in-person learning, where students gather at an appointed time and sit in a room with an instructor. First and foremost, learning is something that happens within a person. What we want our learning programs and courses to do is deliver a learning experience.

A good learning experience is exactly what I am here to help you create with your online courses. Learners take part because they can take part where and when it suits them. They learn at their own pace and feel they're making progress in their daily work.

Learning outcomes with online learning, especially for adult professional learners, can be better than traditional, in-person instructor-led programmes. Set aside for a moment the fact that there is clear market demand as millions of learners around the world sign up for, attend, and complete online learning programmes, research now shows that organisations offering online education to their employees experience 42 per cent growth in revenue.[5]

Other research[6] investigated the impact of online courses on Gen Y (born 1980 to 1994) and Gen Z (born 1995 to 2012) in the workforce.

- Nearly 75 per cent of respondents aged eighteen to twenty-five would participate in a company-sponsored online course
- Among respondents aged eighteen to thirty-four, 50 per cent said access to online courses within a company would positively affect their decision to apply
- More than 50 per cent of respondents aged eighteen to thirty-four reported that access to online courses would affect their decision to stay at a company.

For online learning to be truly effective (i.e. learning that will improve the workplace) we need a shift. Online learning today does not mean the same as e-learning did before the financial crisis in 2008. We can't keep 'teaching for the test'. We cannot simply transpose classroom course material to an online platform and call it a day.

Leaders, trainers, and learning designers in corporate learning and development departments must do three things better:

- Make the best use of current technology
- Understand and focus on learner motivation
- Track metrics that measure learning outcomes

Creating effective online learning programmes that lead to desired behavioural change on the job—achieving change—involves more than tapping into the expertise of leaders in a particular field. Sure, the experts bring credibility and have knowledge worth sharing, but do they know the best way to design learning materials? Did they record a four-hour instructor monologue and serve it up online? Did they create another sort of information dump with a question or two the learner must click at the end to prove they completed the course? Did they build mechanisms into the training programme to help the learner remember, understand, and apply what they've learned?

Ask yourself these two basic questions:

1. Why do I need training in the first place?
2. What do I want the outcomes to be—for each learner and my organisation?

Your answers will form the foundation of strong online learning that results in change.

After that, you'll need to:

- understand basic pedagogy so you can create a learning

experience that's about the learner and not just about the content
- create content, including engaging videos, that attract and keep the learner's attention

The learners should feel:

- that their time is well-spent and that they've enjoyed the training
- that the training improves their experience of work rather than being something the boss told them to do
- inspired and empowered to use new knowledge and tools in their work
- that there is a valuable connection created between theory and how they apply the new knowledge
- a strong connection between the online courses and their daily work.

With just a little help and some tools that are easy to use, you can significantly improve both course quality and learning outcomes. By implementing the *Achieving Change* approach, you can support your people in learning and applying new skills. This will help them to move forward with their great ideas that will bring about more positive change and results, both for them and for your organisation.

THREE

A Model History

❝ With the growing popularity in e-learning, it occurred
to me that the e should mean more than electronic. If
we are going to call it e-learning, shouldn't it be
effective, efficient, and engaging?

— M. David Merrill, pioneer of the first principles of
instruction

U se your imagination for a moment and visualise a time
machine that takes you back 100 years. You visit a
surgeon. You look at the tools he was using a century ago.
The surgeon's operating room has a table, perhaps a chair or stool,
and canvas-wrapped hand tools for cutting, pinching, and stitching.
Then, compare that to the operating rooms of today: computer
screens, fibre-optic scopes, everything high-tech, digital, and bright.

Next you visit a university professor. One hundred years ago,
that professor was standing in front of a chalkboard, lecturing to
students assembled in a lecture hall.

Exit the time machine and return to today. Ah! You still see a professor standing in front of a chalkboard, lecturing to students assembled in that very same lecture hall. The way the professor works is largely unchanged.

Today there is a projector displaying a PowerPoint presentation, and the students are distractedly taking notes on their laptops. Otherwise, despite the speed of change, the shortening of student attention spans, and the opportunities presented by technology, the university lecture hall remains largely unchanged.

How long is the average university lecture? About ninety minutes. What's the perfect length for educational videos, as confirmed by research? Maximum five minutes. Does that not seem like a mismatch between supply and demand?

Much the same can be said for workplace training: in too many instances it has not evolved. If workplaces don't adapt, there won't be any employees to sit around drinking coffee—especially not the kind of employees who are thirsty for learning, always growing and looking for opportunities to benefit them and/or their companies.

A major shift is occurring, however, despite pockets of resistance and denial. The traditional one-way communication model, with the teacher filling knowledge into the heads of students, is giving way to software that fosters collaboration between learners. We have evolved from having a few people developing e-learning platforms in their basements to open source platforms contributing to new business models as well as new thinking. It has significantly evolved from pre-2008 e-learning.

We also know that there is a strong trend towards online learning among institutes of higher education—despite the dogged persistence of lecture-style teaching. Online learning is even now supplementing that style of education, also known as blended learning, working in tandem with long-established traditions to bring new information, in new ways, to new (and even not-so-new) minds. So, although my focus in this book tends toward corporate venues, *Achieving Change* can certainly help anyone looking to develop online learning.

Scorn for SCORM

It's not that long ago that there was no YouTube and there were no Wikis. Instead, we had the *shareable content object reference model,* or SCORM. This is an industry standard that governs how learning systems communicate with each other. It's a technical standard and does not directly address design or pedagogy.

However, a hallmark of SCORM is tracking participation levels of learning participants: how much did they complete? How fast? If there was a question-and-answer section, how did they score? The tracking feature is the main purpose of SCORM. Not learning.

People self-verify when they have watched a video or presentation or completed a module. When they've clicked all the way through, they've "proven" that they completed the course. They are compliant. This isn't an indicator of whether they've actually learned anything. All it proves it that they've clicked through enough pages to get to the end. In this way, the technology does not support the user's real needs, and its design encourages superficial learning only.

A friend of mine worked in a large government organisation where 13,000 people had to be trained to recognise internal bias and thus be more helpful and empathetic to people with disabilities. The cause was important, but the click-and-done training used SCORM to measure success. People went through the screens as fast as they could, answered prescribed questions, and then clicked when they were complete. Very few remembered the information, let alone learned how to use it in their day-to-day jobs. It was purely an information dump, not actual learning. The human resources department got to check off the box in their performance plans that said they were to deliver disability awareness training. Had they instead been required to prove they'd delivered training that actually made a difference to the employees' behaviour back on the job, they'd still have had work to do.

Courses that follow the SCORM model waste a lot of time and money because they don't achieve results. There is a better way.

2008 and Beyond

The 2008 financial crisis forced organisations to think in new ways about e-learning. Faced with lower share values, less revenue, and having to cut their workforce, many organisations looked to online learning as an economical means of training new and existing employees and bringing contract workers up to speed. Gone were the days of hiring training companies to design, develop, and travel all over the place to deliver workshops to small groups of people. Businesses were very financially motivated to get more bang for their buck. Online learning looked to be the way of the future.

MOOCs–Massive Open Online Courses

Canada's University of Manitoba was the first to offer a MOOC in 2005 and had 2,200 participants, although MOOCs didn't really take off until 2012. The first MOOCs after 2012 had hundreds of thousands of participants and were designed to be centralised, linear, and content-based. Since then MOOCs have become:

- decentralised: learners from all around the world can take part
- non-linear: learners can choose for themselves how to order the lessons
- network-based: heavily focused on conversation and exploration over the traditional instructor-led content-based model

In 2012, Harvard University and MIT founded edX and Open edX. In the same year Stanford University started Coursera, and in England, Open University created FutureLearn.

Udacity was the platform that really opened my eyes and got me into the world of online education, and I always recommend new as well as experienced learning designers to participate in at least one of their free online courses to see how great online learning can look like. Back in 2012, Sebastian Thrun had a vision that artificial intelligence (AI) would change the world, and that more people would take their education online. He ran his first experimental course, *Introduction to Artificial Intelligence,* in cooperation with Peter Norvig, Engineering Director at Google. Thrun and Norvig offered the course free of charge and they estimated they would attract between 500 and 800 online users. After the first week the course had 80,000 participants. After two weeks 160,000 learners had enrolled! From this, Udacity was born. Even more inspiring to me is that Thrun, the founder of Udacity and Google X, later gave up his positions, which reduced his salary by 97 per cent, to follow his passion of providing online education for everybody.[1]

This first AI MOOC was a new and different way of thinking about online learning. Now, pioneered by Thrun, online and e-learning often includes more than just content:

- interactions between users
- the employment of problem-centred learning
- real-life case studies
- free for anyone who wants it

Thrun wasn't concerned about whether participants *finished* the course. His goal was simple: provide a means for people to access content that was important to them. Now, if there is internet access, even socio-economically disadvantaged people in developing countries who cannot otherwise attend traditional university can access courses such as water sanitation and farming practices. Achieving change indeed.

People now consider MOOCs a major advancement in higher education. This relatively new technology-enabled approach still has some kinks to work out though. One study found that most MOOCs are of poor instructional design.[2] Further, there is no globally recognised system to measure the quality of a MOOC. While many pioneers in the field serve universities, most corporate designers are still designing their e-learning the old way, wasting time and money, and losing competitive edge. This needs to change.

As of this writing, there are more than 2500 online courses at edx.org, created in cooperation with others who paid significant amounts to put their courses on the platform. There are about twenty million edX users and another forty million Open edX users—and growing.

Stanford University works with other (paying) universities to give online courses through Coursera. The number of participants with Coursera is more than thirty million—and growing.

These different MOOC platforms are all based on a new way of structuring online learning. They use new technologies, include videos of real people in real-life situations, blend learning pedagogy developed over the past 100 years or more, and package everything into an online setting. This marks a new frontier for learning and brings new possibilities for group-work projects within the online system.

While the majority of MOOCs focus on academia, the challenge for you is to elevate your e-learning and incorporate some of the beneficial hallmarks of MOOCs. Videos are not just videos and tests are not just tests. Pedagogy is more important than the technology you employ for your courses.[3]

Achieving Change offers inspiration and instruction, theory, and tactics, as it shows you how you can use the MOOC model together with the latest pedagogical developments to create and deliver powerful online courses. You will see noticeable improvements in on-the-job behaviour, whether your learners are new employees, consultants who need to understand your work procedures, key employees that need to develop their core competencies, or managers moving into a new job.

However, before you can employ the latest pedagogical developments and develop effective online courses, you must first understand how the brain learns. You need to know what a house is before you can use a hammer and saw to build one.

Section I Review

Apply Your New Knowledge

Chances are, you picked up this book with an eye to designing, developing, and/or delivering a online learning course. I invite you now to take a few moments to ponder how to apply the new knowledge you gained in Section I to your situation.

- Why do you need to offer training in the first place?
- What do you hope to achieve with your course(s)?
- What change(s) do you hope to see in your workplace?
- How can this book help you achieve your goals?

Section II: Create

Achieving Change

Step one:
Know The Learning Brain

Step Five:
Assesment for Learning

Step Two:
Initiate Course Development

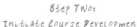

Step Four:
Create the Scripts

Step Three:
Engage the Learner

4. The Four Brain Quadrants

---

66 Learning is the process whereby knowledge is created through the transformation of experience.

David A. Kolb, pioneer of experiential learning

When we learning designers have some understanding of *how* the brain works and learns, we can create a learning experience that stimulates the brain in a way that makes new impressions stick. We can help move information from short-term to long-term memory, which will result in the learner acting in new ways on the job.

(This part of the book can be somewhat theoretical and abstract. But I promise that you will get better results when you've taken the time to understand how the brain learns, and when you use key learning theories, principles, and practices in the design and delivery of your online learning.)

When people learn, you and I included, we activate four parts of the brain:

1. The frontal integrative cortex engages with abstract hypotheses.
2. The aft section of the frontal lobe handles our motor skills and is engaged with active testing.
3. The occipital and parietal lobes toward the back of the brain engage for concrete experiences.
4. The temporal lobe above the brain stem aids with reflective observation.

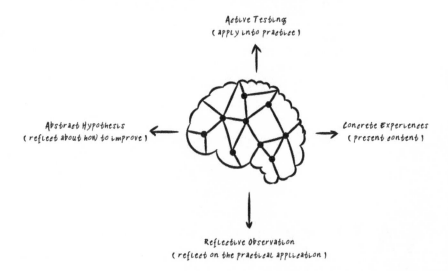

All four parts of the brain are engaged in every learner, even though one area may be preferentially engaged more in one learner as compared to another. A full learning experience will therefore take all the different parts of the brain into consideration.[1]

To turn this understanding of how the brain works into a learning experience, we can follow four approaches that correspond to each part of the brain.

1. Present content, which can be theory or tools for its practical application (frontal integrative cortex).
2. Create a context where the learner can apply the theory or tools into practice (occipital and parietal lobes, aft section of frontal lobe). The theories engaged here include the learning theory of constructivism, which says that learning is an active process.[2]
3. Include scenarios for each learner to reflect on the practical application and assess how it went (temporal lobe). The learning theory here is social constructivism, where learning happens between people and through participation.[3]
4. Include scenarios for the learner to reflect on how they can improve their actions and results next time (temporal lobe). This brings in the learning theory related to reflection and transformative learning, where input moves from short-term memory to long-term and where the learner changes their identity, opinions, and habits.[4]

When you create an online learning program or course, incorporating each of these approaches will engage all parts of the learner's brain and result in better outcomes. Each of these steps is outlined for you in *Achieving Change*.

5. Three Types of Learning

> The principle goal of education in the schools should be creating men and woman who are capable of doing new things, not simply repeating what other generations have done.
>
> Jean Piaget, pioneer of cognitive development theory

A learning experience that enables every learner to store and remember new knowledge involves moving that knowledge from the short-term to the long-term memory. According to Jean Piaget, one of the most acknowledged learning theorists in history, learning happens by putting new information together with existing knowledge through a process of organising new information in the brain.[1] From a neuropsychological perspective, the brain has hundreds of different mental boxes, each of which holds knowledge and understanding within a specific area. When we learn, we can add new content to the boxes or change the current content of the boxes.

The three main types of learning are assimilative, accommodative, and transformative.

Assimilative Learning

Assimilative learning is the principle of "walk before you run" and is the most common type of learning. When a learner receives a chunk of information, the brain immediately determines which box to put the information into.

In an online learning situation, assimilative learning takes place when a learner receives information through video, text or images. If the material is too different from what the learner already knows, the brain will have difficulty finding matching boxes and in most cases the learner won't learn. To help the learner better understand the content, and to make the learning experience smoother, you as a learning designer must create a match—a kind of map—between the learner's existing knowledge and the new knowledge. This is the reason that in primary school math you first had to learn addition and subtraction before you could learn multiplication and division.

Assimilative learning is connected with the learning theory of behaviourism, which simply means that learning happens via receipt of information.

Accommodative Learning

Accommodative learning, on the other hand, takes place when a learner receives information or has an experience that kind of fits a box but is inconsistent with the content already in the box.

When the learner builds new knowledge or new ways of performing tasks that lead to different results than they're used to, the brain will adapt the new knowledge to the already-existing knowledge, and thereby *reconstruct* the existing knowledge.

Accommodative learning is connected with the learning theory of constructivism where learning is an active process. This type of learning can be demanding and requires a learner to be willing to change and adapt. An example of accommodative learning is when Facebook pushes major updates to their interface, and we have to learn to use it in new ways. There is always resistance when this happens because it's too demanding for us to reconstruct our existing knowledge and we don't want to change. Adopting pedagogical principles can stimulate and strengthen this willingness.

Transformative Learning

Transformative learning occurs when people have experiences that change the way they understand the world. The result is a change of opinions, attitudes, and habits. Sometimes this happens through random life experiences. Sometimes it can happen by design.

Jack Mezirow defines transformative learning as learning through which adults learn to think critically instead of taking for granted the assumptions that support a viewpoint. Transformative learning is where adults develop skills to judge, evaluate, and rethink their opinions about what makes sense.

An example of transformative learning can be leadership training. Here leaders not only get information about how to lead (assimilative learning) and alter their mental boxes to accommodate the new information (accommodative learning), but they also must develop new personal traits that make them behave in the best possible way when facing a challenge, even if it conflicts with their existing opinions or habits. They must transform themselves if they are to perform the higher-order thinking needed of true leaders.

Transformative learning is not something that can be taught from instructor to learner. It can be facilitated by an instructor, but the process of altering the mental boxes has to come from within the learner.

The Need for Transformative Learning

Transformative learning is increasingly necessary in adult education, as it has to do with re-training and personal development. It's through a transformative learning experience that we can help the learner develop critical thinking. We want them to develop competencies to judge and evaluate when they face unexpected situations.

If we use the mental boxes analogy to describe transformative learning, it's a reconstruction of a larger number of boxes and their interconnectivity. This is the most demanding type of learning and requires a lot of mental energy from the learner. Therefore, you want to create a learning experience that opens the learner to the possibility of this type of change. This opening becomes possible when the learner reflects critically upon their perceptions and behaviour.

Transformative learning combines two of the four main learning theories: social constructivism, where learning happens between people, and experiential learning, which occurs through reflection by participating, experiencing, reflecting, or abstracting.

By making a connection between the different types of learning and on-the-job activities, we can say a few things with confidence:

- we can gain new knowledge from all types of learning
- assimilative and transformative learning promote new skills
- transformative learning leads to new or enhanced competency

The power in online learning lies within its transformative capacity, in particular the social learning and experiential learning dimensions. We're going to dig a little deeper into each of those now.

6. Social Learning

...there is "huge potential with social learning and we are just scratching the surface."

Andy Parsons, CTO of McKinsey Academy

Contrary to outdated belief, developing knowledge involves an exchange of ideas between people. It's not something you passively receive. We learn from each other. We discuss and negotiate ideas. This exchange and negotiation occur inside relationships. That's social learning.

Social learning is the adolescent's interaction with their friends, family, teachers, as well as their physical environments: nature, city, food, etc. Social learning is the working adult's participation and engagement with their communities of practice in and outside the workplace.

American education psychologist Jerome Bruner said that there is no such thing as real, specific knowledge that all students should have at a given time. Knowledge is culturally and socially determined: it's social exchange that develops and negotiates knowledge.

In an extensive literature review that I conducted when developing this five-step model, I found that using social learning can lead to change. Also, online learning can, if used the right way, be suitable for developing professional skills and competencies. Core elements related to social learning in the pedagogic design of online learning are:

- adopting the view that knowledge is socially constructed
- applying ways to enable the interaction between participants to help them with developing skills and competencies

Situated Learning

Situated learning, connected to social learning, is a concept developed by the internationally-acknowledged educational theorist and practitioner Etienne Wenger-Trayner. It helped broaden the traditional view of the master/apprentice education, where the master has higher knowledge and is more experienced, while the apprentice learns from the master. The theory of situated learning emphasises learning through *interaction*, where the learner co-constructs knowledge within a community of practice (i.e. the workplace, a department, or on-the-job situation). An important aspect of the learner's participation is that the information doesn't have to come from someone with greater knowledge. It can happen through active engagement, which includes activities and interaction with other learners.[1] It's through this social interaction that we create our own meaning. People, therefore, need access to communities or an on-the-job situation to extract meaning from the learning.[2]

Wenger once told a story about being invited to a friend's house for a wine tasting event. Not knowing that much about wine at that time, Wenger was unfamiliar with the expressions used to explain the taste of the wine, how to drink the wine appropriately, and other rules or norms that existed within the wine tasting community. He soon found out that reading the back label of the wine wasn't adequate to describe the taste of the wine when he was among wine enthusiasts. Neither was it an experienced wine enthusiast explaining to others how the wine tasted and what conclusions they should draw from it. In fact, Wenger soon saw how the wine enthusiasts *actively engaged* in tasting the wine together, and how they discussed the taste to *co-create* their own meanings about it. They created and shaped their knowledge and meanings together.

Wenger's experience with the wine tasting can be related to workplace training. To co-create new knowledge, you must have a workplace (the wine tasting event), training content (the wine), and colleagues to discuss the content with in order to create knowledge and new meanings (the wine enthusiasts).

Research also shows that social learning activities like peer assessment, which is a tool where peers can grade and give feedback to each other's assignments, can support development of critical thinking and reflection.[3] Group-work and peer-assessments are inherent in well-designed MOOCs. Educators would be wise to take a page from the MOOC-book and build social learning and peer assessments into all online learning. (We dig deeper into peer assessments in Step Five: Assessment for Learning.)

7. Experiential Learning

---

66 For the things we have to learn before we can do them,
we learn by doing them.

Aristotle

E xperiential learning is learning by doing. It's the hands on,
dig-right-in style of learning that quickly helps the learner
translate the theoretical into the practical. When a learner
can practice what they've just learned, it helps them remember the
new ideas and concepts.

Experiences from practice changes the mindset of the learner,
meaning it's an especially effective learning method for knowledge-
and behaviour-based job functions, such as a leadership role, which
one cannot learn by simply reading about it.[1]

Because of the collaboration elements of experiential learning,
where learners often group together to solve a problem or apply a

concept, engagement increases as each learner feels ownership over the outcome.

Return on investment is high with experiential learning. Multifaceted results include emotions, skills, and knowledge that survive beyond the classroom in a way unrivalled by traditional learning.

As educators, our job is to create opportunities for each learner to apply theory and tools during their own jobs. When this isn't possible, we can do our best to make those theories and tools as tangible as possible by presenting them in case studies.

Experiential learning has the following elements:

- reflection, critical analysis, merging of new information with existing knowledge
- opportunity for the learner to take initiative, make decisions, and be accountable for the results
- opportunities for the learner to engage intellectually, creatively, emotionally, socially, or physically
- the possibility of learning from natural consequences: mistakes and successes

Here are seven benefits of experiential learning.

1. Accelerates learning. Active learning replaces rote memorisation. We use critical thinking, problem solving, and decision making now.
2. Bridges the gap between theory and practice. The difference between hearing a theory in a class and applying that theory to something real in a learner's own life is crucial to learning that theory.
3. Produces demonstrable mindset changes. There are very few learning methods that can have a dramatic

impact on the participant's mindset. Experiential learning is one of them. "Leadership, like swimming, cannot be learned by reading about it."[2]

4. INCREASES ENGAGEMENT LEVELS. Collaborating with peers increases engagement. Immediate involvement in problem-solving boosts levels of ownership.

5. DELIVERS EXCEPTIONAL RETURN ON INVESTMENT (ROI). Experiential learning is personal in nature. When you engage an employee in this kind of learning and apply it to the workplace, the work becomes personal. When people take their work personally, they are more likely to do a better job, and bring their own discretionary efforts to their work. Employees will get a higher return on investment from their efforts, and employers will get a higher return on investment from their employees. Everyone wins.

6. PROVIDES EXACT ASSESSMENT RESULTS. Assessing the effectiveness of benefits to the learner and the company means more effective and efficient courses. Better courses result in better outcomes on the job.

7. ENABLES PERSONALISED LEARNING. This is becoming an increasingly hot topic in the field of corporate training. Instead of students leaving to attend workshops, the workshops come to them. Participants choose what device(s) they'd like to use to access courses, and they set their own learning pace. It's a radical departure from traditional learning and takes it beyond the classroom.

Reflection and Critical Reflection

Reflection is the key to learning from experience. It consciously focusses our attention on what we have learned and merges our new learning with our existing knowledge. However, first we need the experiences to reflect upon. These can be other people's experiences, e.g. from case studies, or our own on-the-job experiences.

Reflection takes place when a learner looks over new knowledge/experiences and thinks about how to use that information to approach a challenge.

Critical reflection, which is a deeper level of reflection, takes place when a learner looks at their own pre-existing premise or basis for a challenge, and considers their opinions, attitudes, and habits as well as why they should be open to changing them. They change their behaviour based on new information.

If we investigate how we can create a learning experience that prompts each learner to store new knowledge in their mental boxes, move knowledge from short-term to long-term memory, and change the current content or behaviour, *reflection* and *critical reflection* are key.

It's through reflection that we learn how to act in certain situations in order to achieve a certain goal.[3] It's through reflection that we learn how and why we should act when we use newly acquired knowledge in practice.

I'll talk in more detail about how to use reflection and critical reflection in online learning in Chapter 21, Effective Assessment.

8. The 70/20/10 Model

---

66 The role of the teacher is to create the conditions for
invention rather than provide ready-made knowledge.

Seymour Aubrey Papert, pioneer of constructionist
learning theory

To help you activate and engage the four brain quadrants
and all key learning theories, I recommend you use the
structure provided by 70/20/10 model. In my experience,
the 70/20/10 model, developed in the 1980s, simply results in superior knowledge transfer and on-the-job application. [1]

- Seventy per cent of a learning experience should happen
  through experience and on-the-job training. It's the
  application of theory that generates the most significant
  learning.
- Twenty per cent of a learning experience should happen
  through group work activities, learning in collaboration
  with other learners.

- Only ten per cent of a learning experience should happen through courseware instruction, such as your videos. These videos should inspire the learner, inform them about theory, illustrate examples, and enable them to perform the on-the-job exercises.

The 70/20/10 formula engages a key mindset during the creation of your online learning programme. It isn't about ensuring you structure your course to fit exactly within each of the 70/20/10 buckets. Instead, use it as a guide. The actual numbers ascribed to what types of content and activities can vary depending on your learning goals, your learners, and your organisation. Some courses are best designed as 70/20/10 while others are best designed as 60/20/20.

Applying the 70/20/10 Learning Model

The smallest portion of the learning, 10 per cent, is providing new information to your learner. The instructional design quality of the content must be excellent—flawless—as it's the foundation for everything else. I'm not talking about the quality of the videos, but the way the content is communicated in the videos. You must present it in a way that the learner can understand and then apply. Here, you will create engaging content that explains complex theory, methods, or approaches in a way that makes it understandable for the learner.

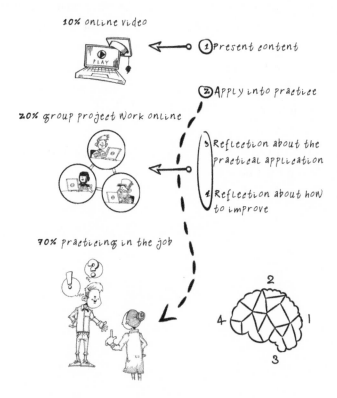

The largest part of learning, 70 per cent, comes from doing assignments and building experience on the job. You want to design content that will help the learner create a plan for, and then use, their newly-acquired knowledge in real life and on the job, enabling them to transform the knowledge into skills. This leads to an actual change, rather than just expanded knowledge.

Group work or discussions will make up the last 20 per cent. Here you will create a structured reflection process that will connect to both the 10 and the 70 per cent. You'll facilitate a social construction of knowledge, where the learner adapts the information they've received and makes it their own. Depending on the medium you use for distributing your course, you can enable effective and user-friendly group work and discussion in an online setting.

You'll notice that the model is called 70/20/10. However, the sections are not always applied in the same way or the same order. The 10 per cent always comes first, but after that you may next engage the 70 per cent and then the 20 per cent, or you may engage the 20 per cent and then the 70 per cent. I encourage you to adapt the principles to fit your specific situation and create a full learning experience. You'll still be using solid pedagogical principles to support maximum learning regardless of whether your circumstances require 10/70/20 or 10/20/70.

However, no matter how you distribute the numbers, it's the concept behind it that matters—that you allow your learner to learn from different experiences.

9. Knowledge, Skills, and Competencies

<blockquote>
"" The only thing worse than training your employees and having them leave is not training them and having them stay.

Henry Ford
</blockquote>

We've looked at how the brain learns, at learning preferences and types. We've examined social learning and experiential learning. And we've touched on reflection and critical reflection. Now it's time to look into the concept of knowledge, skills, and competencies, which are the basic goals of teaching and learning.

By understanding the relationship and distinction between knowledge, skills, and competencies, we can meet each learner's needs and stimulate the type of learning needed to meet the learning goals we set. Knowledge, skills, and competencies are related, as competencies build on top of skills, and skills on top of knowledge. Think about what competencies you want your learner to achieve, and what skills and knowledge it requires. This will set the foundation for your course's learning goals and the content needed to achieve these goals.

Knowledge   Skills   Competencies

Knowledge

Knowledge is the ability to understand and remember. Knowledge involves cognitive and theoretical understanding as opposed to practical application. It's about understanding and remembering. You can get knowledge from books, online research, documentaries, etc. Having knowledge of something doesn't necessarily mean you are automatically able to apply it. For instance, reading books about how to play the piano does not mean you can play the piano.

Skills

You have a skill when you have the ability to apply and analyse. Skills are learned behaviours. You gain skills by doing. You train, and you practice, and you practice some more until you become skilled at something. The "something" can be cognitive, technical, or social. Cognitive skills would include things like being able to understand and analyse scholarly works or being able to stay focussed on a task. A technical skill might be typing quickly and accurately. A social skill might be knowing how to actively listen to others.

Competencies

Competencies are more than just knowledge or skill, they include behaviours, abilities, and knowledge that's critical to the execution of a skill. They can be intellectual, personal, social, or emotional. A competency is the ability to evaluate and create.

Picture a brain surgeon. She has a tremendous amount of knowledge about the brain and has developed skills by practicing cutting and stitching for years. She is knowledgeable and skilled, yet once she gets into the operating theatre, she must also bring her competencies of analytical thinking, technical ability, and leadership to the table if she is to be a truly effective surgeon. She needs to be able to immediately analyse, evaluate, and act if something unpredictable happens.

Step one :
Know The Learning Brain

Step One Review

Apply Your New Knowledge

- What competencies do you want your learner to have? And what skills and knowledge do those competencies require?
- What does your learner already know? How can you connect the new knowledge you're helping them learn to that existing knowledge?
- What steps can you take to ensure this new information has a place to land, e.g., an existing mental box?
- How might you design your course to be inclusive of your learner's workplace?
- How can you facilitate discussion with and between learners, so they co-create knowledge together?
- How can you incorporate the 70/20/10 approach and what might be the appropriate ratio for your course?

Achieving Change

Step one :
Know The Learning Brain

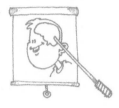

Step Five:
Assesment for Learning

Step Two:
Initiate Course Development

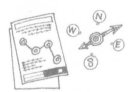

Step Four:
Create the Scripts

Step Three:
Engage the Learner

10. Learning Goals

> ❝ There are only two ways to influence human behaviour:
> you can manipulate it, or you can inspire it.

Simon Sinek, author of *Start With Why*

An online learning course must create a purpose for the learner and motivate them by telling them *why* it's important for them to learn the new knowledge, and which results it will help them achieve. As a designer of online learning, you want to remove the barriers to accepting *why* the knowledge is important before your learner will be open to learning the content itself, which is the *what*. In addition, you must also include a hefty dose of *how* to use the knowledge, so they will be able to get the promised results.

Your goal is to create an online learning experience that enables learners to analyse, evaluate, apply, and create. To achieve this goal, you must motivate your learner to practice the new knowledge or tools in real life. The connection to real life will give the learner experience which, through a facilitated reflection process, will help them develop new skills and competencies that they can use to make a difference on their job.

In the world of corporate education, here's a conversation I have had repeatedly with course designers, managers, and executives:

"What's the aim of your training?" I ask.

"To have employees understand and remember what I teach them," is the inevitable reply.

"Would you also like them to use new knowledge and tools in their daily work?"

"Well, yes, of course." They always look rather perplexed, as though it was silly of me to ask.

"So, why is the learning designed only for understanding and remembering... but not doing?"

"Um..."

Exactly.

The course and the course material contained within it are not the be all and end all. We, as learning designers, must help the learner become interested in what we're teaching as well as the process of learning.

And so, before you're ready to dig into creating your learning goals, we need to talk about the role of the SME.

11. Subject Matter Experts

> An integrated course design requires a significant investment in time, energy, and thought.

Dr. L. Dee Fink

E very student on the planet probably realises that not everyone who knows a subject well will be a good teacher. The greatest barrier, and the most difficult mindset to shift, is the mistaken idea that you can foster learning through courses based solely on information dump. The challenge that any SME faces is that they often become blind to how much they know. They forget that others don't have the same foundation, so they'll info-dump about things that the learner doesn't yet have a basic understanding of. They may forget to include something important, because they think it's basic common knowledge when it's not.

Remember assimilative learning? There needs to be a pre-existing mental box for new information, otherwise there will be no new learning. For this reason, and to help shine a bright light on any SME blind spots, they must describe everything thoroughly.

Your role is to extract theoretical knowledge and tools from the SME's head—or from your own head if you're the SME—and transfer these into a learning experience that helps people achieve results.

However, cooperating with a knowledgeable expert can sometimes be a challenge. Many experts are passionate about what they do, and they think that everybody else shares the same passion. Some are too close to their subject, unable to be objective about what's important. This is where a learning designer can get overwhelmed with information and end up developing a course that only touches on *what* the knowledge or tools being taught are about, not *why* they're important or *how* to apply them in practice. To the expert, it's so obvious as to why the material is important that they can't even conceive of having to spell it out to others—yet that's exactly what they need to do.

The SME's passion for the topic is a wonderful thing. However, it doesn't play a role in effective learning outcomes. In fact, I have seen trainers and instructors who are so passionate about the material that they forget all about learning design. Without proper knowledge of, and consideration for, how the human brain works, and how to design effective online learning, passion alone will not lead to high learning outcomes.

Now, let's look at how to create a connection between content and the learner to create a learning experience that empowers learning.

12. What, Why, and How

> The purpose of adult education is to help them to learn,
> not to teach them all you know and thus stop them from
> learning.

Carl Rogers, pioneer of the humanistic approach

A s you start your course development, you'll produce an overview of the course. This will help you to reflect about key elements to include in your script and ensure that you are heading in the right direction. (We'll be coming back to this in Step Four: Create the Scripts.) In doing so, you want to identify situational factors such as:

- Learning goals: what should the learner be able to do?
- Content: what knowledge must they have to achieve the learning goals?
- Activities: what will the learner need to do in order to apply the knowledge?

- Tools: what tools can the learner use to carry out the learning activities?
- Reflection: what tasks will create reflective processes and group work discussions?
- Assessment: what assessment mechanisms will help assess whether each learner has achieved the learning goals, and if not, how will I get them onto the right path?

Once you've considered these high-level concepts, you can dig deeper into situational factors.

CONTEXT OF THE LEARNING SITUATION:

- What's the level of the course?
- What's the work effort required?
- What physical elements of the learning environment will affect the course?
- What learning expectations are placed on this course?

NATURE OF THE SUBJECT:

- Is this subject primarily theoretical, practical, or a combination?
- Have there been controversies or recent changes within the field?

CHARACTERISTICS OF THE LEARNER:

- What prior knowledge and experiences does the learner have relevant to this subject?
- What are the learner's goals and expectations of the course?

CHARACTERISTICS OF THE TEACHER:

- What beliefs and values does the SME have about teaching and learning?
- What level of knowledge does the SME have about the subject?
- What are the SME's teaching strengths and weaknesses?

The What, Why, and How of Learning Design

As a learning designer beginning to develop a course, you will consider the questions *what*, *why*, and *how*. This process is what enables you to create a structure for your course, so you are able to develop content and scripts for your videos. It's natural for learning designers to first think about *what* the learner has to know, and then afterwards think about *why* they have to learn it and *how* they can apply it. The tools I use for this process are sticky notes, a whiteboard, and a document, either Word or Google Docs. Get started by writing down your answers to these questions:

- *What* are the learning goals?
- *Why* are they important?
- *How* can I support the learning process?

What Are the Learning Goals?

The first thing you'll want to do is to identify the knowledge you want to teach in your course. Think of the knowledge as *what* your learner has to learn. Brainstorm and write all the answers down on sticky notes. Then organise the answers into categories and put them up on a whiteboard.

Why are the Learning Goals Important?

Next, describe *why* the knowledge is important for the learner. *Why* motivates the learner to engage. You want the learner to understand why they should take part in the course, and you want to create a hunger in each learner so that when they finish one video, they're eager to watch the next.

This step forces you and the SME to reflect upon the chosen knowledge from the "what" and to structure their thoughts better. It's very common at this stage that the SME will remove or add some of the identified knowledge from the "what," perhaps even coming to some new conclusions. This is fine.

When I work with a new client to begin course development, I ask them why they think it's important for employees to learn what's going to be offered in the course. Almost always, the first answer they give me is, "Because it's their job." While technically true, no learner on the planet will be motivated to learn *because it's their job*. This answer is, in fact, demotivating. We should instead focus on communicating what difference it will make for them in their daily work, how they will benefit, what it will be possible for them to achieve, and what pain points it will help them avoid.

How Can I Support the Learning Process?

For each *what* and *why*, we try to see if there is a tool that can support the process. A tool could be a handout, a practical hands-on exercise, a video that illustrates how to carry out the *what*, or even something as simple as a brochure. Be aware, however, that you might not be able to come up with a specific tool for every *what*. That's okay.

Whenever possible, for each *what*, give a tool and instructions, in the form of an example, to show how to use the tool.

This will move the tool from theoretical to tangible, creating a more direct line to learning about the subject at hand.

You'll want to consider the tools you'll use to help the learner apply the knowledge by asking the following questions.

- How can the learner use the newly acquired knowledge?
- What activities can help the learner put the knowledge into practice?
- What tools can help the learner practice the activities?

Once this exercise is complete, you'll want to record the what, why, and how from the whiteboard into a document.

TOPIC ONE

1. What
2. Why
3. How

Topic Two

1. What
2. Why
3. How

Repeat this process for each of your topics. This document will become the foundation for your course content, which we'll dig deeper into in Step Four: Create the Scripts.

You will know this phase is complete when both you and the subject-matter expert feel that you have a great overview, and everything is covered. At this point, you may experience an "Aha!" moment (or several) where the material and the ideas for the learning design suddenly seem to fall into place and make more sense. That's normal. After finishing the *what, why, how* process, you will be able to create reflection activities, which I will talk more about in Step Five: Assessment for Learning.

Errors and Misconceptions

Watch for these common errors and misconceptions that often crop up during this phase.

- *WHAT* WITHOUT *WHY*. Many learning designers are tempted to focus only on learning goals: the *what* without the *why*. Don't underestimate the importance of explaining the *why*, which has a significant influence on learner motivation.
- No "HOW-TO-USE" INSTRUCTIONS. It's a mistake to believe that you don't need to provide how-to-use instructions for every tool. Instructions do more than help each learner use the tool. They clear the path to learning what you're trying to teach, and also help them

understand how to apply the knowledge back on the job and in real life.

- NOT LEARNER-CENTRIC. You want to ensure you are keeping the learner at the centre of the training. Why and how people learn is just as important as what they learn.

Step Two:
Initiate Course Development

Step Two Review

Apply Your New Knowledge

- What is it that your learner wants and/or needs to know? (These are the learning goals.) Take your time to explore this fully.
- Why should your learner want and/or need to know what you want to teach them? What's in it for them? What will motivate them?
- Which tools will help your learners to apply what you're teaching them?
- What form of instruction do you think will best fit each tool?
- How can you get your learners working together, with one another? Make room for social learning.
- Who is the SME? If it's you, how can you ensure that you don't fall into the traps that so commonly befall SMEs? If it's not you, how can you help your SME?

Achieving Change

one :
Know The Learning Brain

Step Five:
Assesment for Learning

Step Two:
Initiate Course Development

Step Four:
Create the Scripts

Step Three:
Engage the Learner

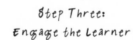

13. Connecting Content & Learner

> ❝ If you talk to a man in a language he understands, that goes to his head. If you talk to him in his language, that goes to his heart.
>
> Nelson Mandela

O ur greatest task as learning designers is to create a connection between the content and the learner, so the learner can and will learn.

There's a lot of great information at the library. Why don't we all just send people to the library? Or tell them to do an internet search? It's because the library offers only *some* of the 10 per cent in our 70/20/10 model. The library won't be especially good at catching the learner's attention, and the information it provides access to will certainly not be engaging for most of your learners.

When developing online learning course content, you want the *learner* at its centre, not the content. We want always to present material in a way that truly speaks to the learner.

It means thinking constantly about how to communicate so the learner can understand—and apply. It will take you a lot of mental work, as a learning designer, to keep stepping into the learner's shoes and not just keep focussing on content.

The first and most basic technique for engaging your learner is *to talk directly to the learner* instead of the masses. If you are the instructor or presenter, it's easy to think that the content you present will go out to hundreds or even thousands of students. However, the reality is that each learner in an online context engages one-on-one with you. It's just you (or the instructor, or the person speaking in the video) and them. They want a personal learning experience. You want to give it to them. Here are a few of the basic rules to make this happen:

- Always talk directly to the learner as if he or she was standing just in front of you.
- Use "you" instead of "they" or "people."
- You want to give the learner a good reason to spend their time engaging with your content. They must see a need. When you create verbal and visual information that inspires the learner to add the knowledge to their own mental boxes in a way that makes it meaningful for them, you're helping create long-lasting knowledge. You're creating learning that instigates change. Your engagement roadmap should look something like this:
- Present the content, such as theory or tools.
- Create a context where each learner can apply the theory or tools in practice.
- Have the learner reflect on the application and how it went.
- Have the learner reflect on how they can improve their actions next time.

Engaging the learner helps ensure they're actively involved. In this step, you'll consider and engage the four parts of the learning brain, you'll incorporate the 70/20/10 approach, and you'll use a variety of pedagogical principles to motivate the learner and stimulate reflection. And through it all, the learner will be at the centre of the course development process, right from when you brainstorm about how to create your course.

14. Creating Engaging Content

>   Where my reason, imagination or interest were not
> engaged, I would not or I could not learn.

Winston Churchill

When I design learning programmes that lead to actual change, I'm guided by four principles that help ensure a high learning outcome for the learner. These principles integrate some of the most significant learning theory and research from the time of Aristotle until today and they help ensure I'm taking the learner's experience into consideration. They reflect the development in learning theory over time, adding new perspectives to earlier theories, rather than substituting the new theories and throwing out the old. You will use these four principles to create engaging content in your course.[1]

1. *Problem-based*: solving real-world problems promotes learning.

2. *Demonstration*: demonstration of new knowledge promotes learning.
3. *Application*: applying new knowledge in the course promotes learning.
4. *Integration*: integrating new knowledge into the real world promotes learning.

Principle One: Problem-Based

Your task: present a problem and ask the learner to solve it.

When a learner accesses the context of real-world problems, learning happens. We learn far better when we are engaged in solving problems and building knowledge. Lectures and other information dumps that need to be memorised don't lead to learning outcomes that foster behavioural change. That requires the learner to assume ownership, and that only occurs if the problems are interesting, relevant, and engaging.

What constitutes a "problem?" It's a whole task comprising a range of activities, not just components. The task must reasonably represent a situation (problem) the learner will encounter in real life.[2]

Structure your problems so the learner will work through the least complex through to the most complex in a "progression of interrelated tasks" that reflect the reality they will face on the job.[3]

Depending on the learning environment and the possibilities for interacting with practice, problem-centred learning can occur in two ways:

- through examination of case studies
- by solving a problem at the workplace

A case study can give a learner a starting point. It could be a story of a person who is in a certain situation that must somehow resolve. You could then present theory and follow that with an assignment requiring them to connect the case study and the theory, and to solve the problem using the theory.

Conversely, you or the learner can find a problem that exists in the workplace that you can solve using the new theory.

This problem-solving approach will make the learning experience more engaging and relevant to the learner.

Principle Two: Demonstration

Learning something new can quickly become an abstract experience. It's hard for the learner to figure out how to apply theory in their day-to-day jobs. If they find it too difficult or can't see a connection to their own work, you risk losing their attention. It helps to show them how to do that.

Demonstration is an effective principle in learning, especially in online learning. This principle highlights the importance of showing the learner how to apply theory or a skill rather than merely presenting them with information about what to do.[4]

There are two types of demonstration: behavioural and cognitive. Behavioural demonstrations show how to do things. Cognitive demonstrations articulate *why* the learner should use the knowledge/skill that's the focus of the demonstration.

Demonstration can take one of three possible forms:

1. An instructor or interviewee telling a story or showing how to use a model
2. Animation with storytelling or explanation
3. Filming a real-life situation

Allow the learner to watch a demonstration or portrayal of the new knowledge or skill through illustrative examples. Guide them to something specific to help them relate context of the new knowledge or skill you want them to learn.

Some learners don't need a demonstration, depending on how their brains process and assimilate new information. However, demonstration is an effective tool for ensuring that everyone taking the course can translate theory into practice.

For example, one person might be able to figure out how to juggle three oranges just from having someone explain how. Another person might need to see someone else juggle the oranges before being able to do it themselves. Someone else might want both instruction and demonstration. All three people will need lots of practice.

You will enhance the effectiveness of your course:

- when the learner sees examples of good practices and even poor practices, depending on the content
- when the demonstration is consistent with what you're teaching
- when you give examples to illustrate general information or an organisational structure[5]

Research shows that presenting examples is more effective than merely presenting information and that it promotes better learning. Multiple representations are even better for demonstration. Getting to see theory applied in various ways means something is more likely to stick. Multiple approaches can call upon a range of intelligences, skills, and interests.

How you decide which type of demonstration to use will depend on the content itself.

Principle Three: Application

Applying new knowledge or skill to real-world tasks is a necessary condition for effective learning. Adding practice to information and examples increases learning. The principle of application—where the learner applies the theory into practice as a part of the learning experience—is one of the most effective pedagogic principles for making this happen. When you design and/or lead an online learning course, you want to be sure to create a connection between theory and practice.

You can facilitate application by including a case for the learner to solve, or by setting them explicit tasks to solve in their daily practice. In situations where it's not possible to involve cases to solve, you can show examples that are closely related to their practice, allowing them to compare the examples to their own practice and apply the knowledge or theory to their work.

Requiring learners to answer multiple-choice questions can be part of the application process, however it isn't enough on its own to generate a learning process that results in behaviour change on the job. Instead, look for a variety of ways they can apply the new information.

When preparing the problems or case scenarios for the learner to apply their new knowledge, it's not enough to give a single problem or scenario. Learners sometimes need multiple scenarios and a range of problems to guide them.

Principle Four: Integration

Where the principle of application was concerned with applying new knowledge or skills *within the context of the course*, the principle of integration occurs when a learner integrates, or transfers, the new knowledge or skills *into everyday life*. In this way, application and integration overlap somewhat, as solving problems forms a part of both on the path to enhancing learning.

To foster integration, include problems for the learner to solve that inspires them to use (integrate) the new knowledge and skills they've gained from the course. Reflection and discussion provide a focus on how the theory worked when they applied it in practice, either in a real-life situation or working with a case.[6]

You can encourage integration through assignments that include reflective questions.

Keep in mind that we want the learner to reflect about them-selves, so they can be open to new learning. When a learner reflects about theory it helps them to move the new learning into their mental boxes.

- How does this theory fit with your personal beliefs about ___?
- What similar experiences have you encountered in the past?
- How does this relate to your current work?

Reflection is the key to learning from experience—experiential learning—because it consciously focusses a learner's attention on what they have learned and thus consolidates it.

Experiential learning has all these elements:

- reflection, critical analysis, and synthesis
- opportunities to take initiative, make decisions, and be accountable for the results
- opportunities to engage intellectually, creatively, emotionally, socially, or physically
- potential to learn from natural consequences, mistakes, and successes

When the learner shows improvement in their skills, can defend their knowledge, and modify the new knowledge to work in their daily lives, you know they have fully integrated the information.

Engaging Content in Action

Knowledge is worth nothing if you are unable to *apply* the knowledge you've gained. Application is all about helping the learner translate their new knowledge into achieving change.

Ideally, your course should follow a pattern like this one:

1. REVEAL WHY IT'S IMPORTANT to learn the material. We learn better when we see the task that we'll be able to do or the problem we'll be able to solve because we've completed a module or course.
2. OFFER GUIDANCE AND FEEDBACK. Help the learner activate existing knowledge and skills and build extra levels on top of that. Guide the learner when they're solving a task and understand they're not yet ready for a sink-or-swim approach. In the early stages, you may need to give considerable support. The learner's skills will gradually improve as the course progresses. For example, to master a complex problem, students gain from starting with a less complex problem. Only when they master the first problem will they be ready to take on problems with more complexity. Provide them with feedback on their progress as this will make them feel that they are learning, which for most learners is the greatest motivator for learning itself. Most learning theorists recognise feedback as the most effective type of learner guidance.[7]
3. DEMONSTRATE HOW TO USE THE SKILL or knowledge in practice. We learn better when we can see others applying the material, whether through animation, illustration, interviews, or storytelling.
4. SET A REAL-LIFE TASK. Cognitive psychology research suggests that we learn better when actively engaged in a problem or task. There can even be a progression of problems to solve, where the learner solves a series of problems that they can explicitly compare with one another. It's good practice to make the first problem in a sequence be a worked example that shows students the type of task that they will learn to complete.
5. HELP THE LEARNER INTEGRATE the new information

into their own lives. Get them to reflect on how they can apply the material on the job, or even in their personal life. Create a plan for integrating the material into the learner's job. You or the learner's manager can help them create an individual development plan.

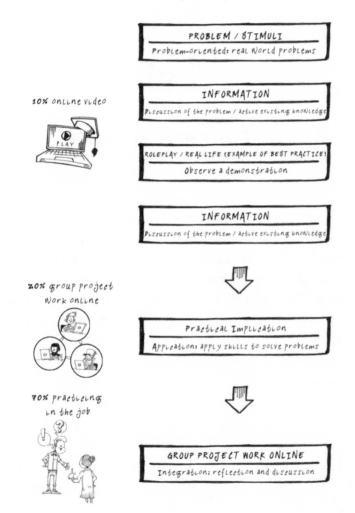

PROBLEM / STIMULI
Problem-oriented: real world problems

10% online video

INFORMATION
Discussion of the problem / active existing knowledge

ROLEPLAY / REAL LIFE (EXAMPLE OF BEST PRACTICE)
Observe a demonstration

INFORMATION
Discussion of the problem / active existing knowledge

20% group project work online

Practical Implication
Application: apply skills to solve problems

70% practicing in the job

GROUP PROJECT WORK ONLINE
Integration: reflection and discussion

15. Ethos, Pathos, and Logos

> Of the modes of persuasion furnished by the spoken word there are three kinds. The first kind depends on the personal character of the speaker [Ethos]; the second on putting the audience into a certain frame of mind [Pathos]; the third on the proof, or apparent proof, provided by the words of the speech itself [Logos]. Persuasion is achieved by the speaker's personal character when the speech is so spoken as to make us think him credible.
>
> *Aristotle*

Ethos, Pathos, and Logos describe and dictate how you establish credibility, engage in storytelling, and include facts.

- ETHOS: you as the presenter are reliable, trustworthy, competent, and credible.
- PATHOS: what you communicate evokes an emotionally

appropriate response.

- LOGOS: what you communicate is logical and rational.

Ethos, Pathos, and Logos help you to structure your online learning course to support and empower learners in understanding and enjoying the content of the lecture. When they do that, they are paying attention and they are engaged. Win, win!

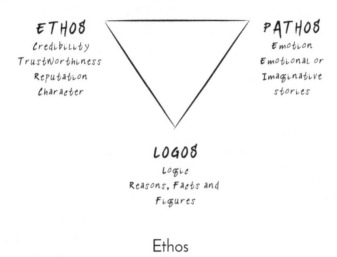

ETHOS
Credibility
Trustworthiness
Reputation
Character

PATHOS
Emotion
Emotional or
Imaginative
stories

LOGOS
Logic
Reasons, Facts and
Figures

Ethos

Ethos deals with the character of the presenter, whose intent is to appear credible and trustworthy.

Aristotle said there are three pre-requisites to appearing credible: competence, good intention, and empathy.

The lecturer transmits their Ethos via their self-portrayal, through both nonverbal and verbal factors.

Factors that can further influence Ethos may include clothing, vocabulary, colloquialisms, slang, and other social aspects like rank and popularity. These factors can affect the appearance and reception of the presenter.

The goal of the presenter, in terms of Ethos, is to express credibility and authenticity about their character, not about their arguments or viewpoints (yet). The information retrieved from one mode of persuasion must be in harmony or congruence with each of the others. I remember seeing a video in a MOOC about zoology: the zookeeper was sitting in the zoo in his work clothes with an animal enclosure behind him. He appeared authentic. However, if he had been wearing a suit and tie, he would not have been in harmony with his surroundings. His credibility would have suffered.

There are also social aspects to credibility. For instance, identity and membership in a group. When a presenter appears to be a member of the learner group, they can gain credibility more easily. Research in leadership suggests "that to gain credibility among followers, leaders must try to position themselves among the group rather than above it."[1]

BODY LANGUAGE

Body language isn't formally a part of language, per se, but elements like facial expression, posture, gait, coughs, yawns, hand or head movements, gaze, and so on, do convey information to others. You may not always be aware that you are sending information, and you are never in charge of how another person interprets that information, but nevertheless, it plays an important role in our interactions.

Body language is known for reflecting the emotional state of a person. It contributes to the affectations of the listener/observer and influences the entire process of communication and learning. Our main concern should be that the collective signal we send—deliberate language and body language—is congruent. People will attribute certain characteristics, such as competence, sympathy, and honesty based on things like posture, how you move in relation to another person, touching behaviours and such. Sometimes movement behaviour has more weight than even visual appearance.

Facial expression includes all moving and fixed parts of the human head that are visible while looking directly at the other person. They can transmit the emotional state of one person and influence another. So, when appearing on camera, a smiling presenter will appear engaged and engaging for a learner. Even with regular coaching and reminders about smiling, most novice on-camera presenters realise they need to smile a lot more when they see themselves in recordings. That said, if your smile appears forced or unnatural, the receiver will know it, and you'll seem insincere and erode your apparent trustworthiness. Find a way of increasing your smiles, while keeping them real.

Facial expression also involves eye contact. The eye contact between the speaker and the camera is a key aspect. A teleprompter is helpful for maintaining eye contact when presenting.

VOICE

With voice, the main points to consider are volume, tonality, speed, and rhythm. Some vocal aspects, such as volume and speed, allow a presenter to create variety. You can use variations to emphasise certain aspects of a presentation and to create a more dynamic performance. Pausing is one of the most effective speech variations. It's used differently and for multiple reasons: emphasis, drama, enhancing interest, enabling thinking, raising tension, and so on. If you speak quickly you may create a more intensive emotional effect, but add breaks between key messages or after asking a question so the learner has an opportunity to think and reflect.

Think about a recent business meeting you attended; if you have to digest an important message or think about a question, you want time to reflect. Your brain is already missing the next lines because it's saying, "What? What did he just say?" Build in those breaks and give your learner time to absorb what you're teaching them.

I usually recommend that presenters do the following:

- Speak quickly. A video becomes boring to watch if the speaker is too slow. That's why some video platforms allow the learner to speed up video by as much as two times the original recorded speed. They can absorb the information faster than it can be spoken.

- Vary tone of voice to make the presentation more engaging.
- Pause between sentences to allow the learner time to reflect.
- Use hand gestures and be aware of body language.
- Insert a short pause after asking the learner a question. If the question has an answer, use a short pause before giving the answer: *"So, what does this mean? <pause> It means you can..."* or *"How do you solve this? <pause> You can solve it by..."*

Pathos

Pathos is about stimulating certain emotions in the learner in order to persuade them to make desired judgements. Triggering Pathos will make the learner excited about getting this new set of knowledge or skills, or afraid that they'd be missing out if they don't. Pathos makes a learner want to learn because they see the learning as relevant to them. Pathos means the learner wants to learn the material and that they'll feel great about learning it.

Pathos is a form of persuasion, and stories are excellent vehicles for Pathos. When we listen to stories, we get involved in the tale and are more open to the lessons contained in them.

Storytelling is part of the daily communication experience. It gives a personal touch, can create curiosity in the audience, and even make examples more vivid. It can also create a more casual environment during a speech.

The persuasive effect of storytelling has long been known. The Roman rhetorician Quintilian mentioned that narration should not only give new information, but that it should convince the audience. A story allows a speaker to raise emotions naturally, also to present a solution to the problem in an indirect manner as an outcome.

Furthermore, stories have a strong connection with peoples' childhood memories, thus listening to a story reduces the possibility and/or willingness to at once respond critically towards the content. From parables to fairy tales, we've been teaching by storytelling for about as long as we've had language. Pathos is a big reason for its effectiveness.

Integrate Pathos into your online learning courses to engage the learner and to provide incentives for them to want to follow the course. Pathos will also help you create a *need* in each learner. For example, you can interview a person who tells a story. Or you can tell a story about a person. Your aim is to create a need to know with respect to how to avoid having a similar negative experience, or how to achieve a specific result.

Logos

Logos is about appealing to logic, relying on the audience's intelligence, and offering credible evidence to support an argument. In other words, the lecturer presents an argument that appears sound to the audience.

Evidence presented should include the following:

- Facts. These are valuable because they are not debatable; they are the truth.
- Examples. They can describe events or circumstances that the audience can relate to in their own lives, even giving an "aha" experience.
- Precedents. Specific examples, historical, and personal. They show real-life evidence of truth.
- Authority. That authority must be up-to-date and qualified to judge the topic. An authority figure can give an interview where they give evidence.
- Deductive/inductive reasoning. Deductive reasoning picks apart evidence to reach conclusions, while

inductive reasoning involves adding logical pieces to the evidence to reach conclusions.

Address Logos continuously throughout the content, not only during the introduction. Including facts and/or numbers helps to pique each learner's interest and make sense of the information because it's logical to follow. Content relating to Logos can be facts, figures, data, and the like. Remember to combine it with Ethos to make the effect stronger. Here's what I mean:

- Logos alone: "A survey showed that ..."
- Logos and Ethos: "Research conducted by Harvard University showed that..."
- Logos and Ethos: "A survey with more than ten thousand respondents showed..."

When using Logos, you want—as with anywhere else in the course—to have the learner as your focus and speak directly to them. Build facts and numbers into the conversations with learners.

Here are two examples to demonstrate the point.

1. *Did you know that you can improve your sales by up to 80 per cent if you follow this five-step sales approach developed by Stanford University? Let's look into how you can use this new approach yourself, and how you can use it to increase your own sales at once.*
2. *Research shows that when following a five-step sales approach, sales personnel can improve their sales by up to 80 per cent.*

Example one is much better as it's learner-centred and speaks directly to the learner.

Ethos and Logos are usually the easier of the three concepts to invoke. Lecturers, both onsite and online, are often experts in their field and therefore tend to have a strong focus on Ethos (presenting themselves and talking about their professional background) and on Logos (communicating theories, scientific facts, factual data, statistics, etc.). However, they tend to forget about Pathos and the importance of "putting the audience into a certain frame of mind" that will touch their emotions and make them feel that *they want to learn*.[2]

Step Three Review

Apply Your New Knowledge

- Check your language: are you using words like *everyone, you guys,* and *people?* Make learning personal by using words like *you, I,* and *we* instead.
- How can the knowledge you're teaching be used to solve a real-world problem for your learner? Can you find or create a case study?
- What are some other ways you can help your learner apply the new knowledge?
- How can you incorporate into your course exercises or activities that help your learner to integrate their new knowledge and skills into daily life?
- How can you encourage integration so learners can help each other?
- Write down several questions for the learner that will encourage them to reflect on how to apply the new

material on the job and even in their personal life (if applicable).

- How can you include Ethos, Pathos and Logos?

Achieving Change

Step one :
Know The Learning Brain

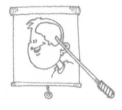

Step Five:
Assesment for Learning

Step Two:
Initiate Course Development

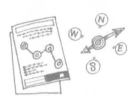

Step Four:
Create the Scripts

Step Three:
Engage the Learner

16. Structuring Your Content

Description begins in the writer's imagination, but should finish in the reader's.

Stephen King

Y ou understand the learning brain, the *what, why,* and *how* approach to initiating content, and ways to engage the learner. Now it's time to roll up your sleeves and begin to create the content.

You want to extract the knowledge from the heads of you or your SME and turn it into scripts that engage the learner and foster learning.

You want your learner to spend their mental energy learning, not trying to figure out what you mean with the things you say. Writing effective scripts will help you to structure your knowledge and communicate it clearly.

Your scripts are the building blocks of your video content. In almost all cases, online learning involves presentation of course content via video. I will talk about what to do if you are not able to create video, however for the most part assume that a great online learning experience involves video. Later we will talk about the benefits of using a teleprompter, but for now, understand that you'll be using your scripts to read voiceover or speak directly into the camera to create videos. More on this shortly.

Before you write your scripts, know that you'll likely make changes to your scripts several times before they are ready for filming. Why? Because the process of writing scripts will also be a learning journey for you—as you will learn more about your own content. You will come back to each script, rewriting and simplifying and in the process making it more precise. In other words, you'll get to understand your content so well that you can explain it simply.

When you create your course content, put yourself in the shoes of your learner. Think about *why* they should pay attention to what you say. What will make them start and then continue watching your videos? The answer is to make clear for them what they will be able to achieve or do with the new knowledge. It's the goal that's important for your learner, and the knowledge is simply a means to achieve that goal.

Your course will have two types of goals: an *overall goal* for participating in the whole course and *partial goals* for each topic within your course.

The overall goal should be presented in the introduction, while the partial goals should be presented within each topic of the course.

Course Introduction

In order to create a meaningful introduction for your learner, you should include five things, and in this order:

1. Set the goal
2. Establish credibility
3. Explain what they'll learn
4. Explain how they'll learn it

5. Explain how they'll be assessed

Depending on the size of your course, your introduction can be in one or more videos. However, I advise you to keep it simple and focus your energy on setting the goal. That's what's important for the learner.

1. SET THE GOAL. You have to explain to your learner what they'll be able to achieve or do with what they'll learn from participating in your course. This will do two things: get their attention and help them connect with their *why* for taking the course.

2. ESTABLISH CREDIBILITY. The next step is to tell them that you can help them achieve their goals. You do this by introducing yourself, or the instructor, using Ethos. Ask them about any degrees they may have, any books written, the work they've done, explore their level of passion for the subject, and anything else that you think might help establish trust and rapport with the learner. This is what sets up credibility. If the learner likes and trusts the instructor, they are more likely to be open to learning from them.

3. EXPLAIN WHAT THEY'LL LEARN. Explain what you'll teach and what they'll learn. At this point you will have confirmed for the learner that they do, in fact, want to achieve the goal and hopefully they'll also think, *"This is the teacher to help me achieve it."*

4. EXPLAIN HOW THEY'LL LEARN. Explaining how your learner is going to learn and what they should expect through the process helps them feel safe about their learning journey.

Imagine going on a hike. You come across a deep and wide crevice and it's right in your path. You look down, way down, and you feel fearful about how you're going to get to the other side. You have two hiking instructors with you. The first one tells you to simply get to the other side, which you don't find helpful at all. The other hiking instructor says, "To cross this crevice, we'll first tie a safety rope around each of our waists, so we are connected." Then the instructor points at some rocks protruding from the crevice wall. "We'll step on that rock, then that one, and there's the third step.

That will get us down, and then we can start to climb up the other side."

Your learner will feel uncertain about how they're going to get across their knowledge crevice. You want to tell them how they are going to get safely to the other side. This will include explaining the upcoming activities, like watching videos, doing exercises or on-the-job activities, or group work projects.

5. EXPLAIN HOW THEY'LL BE ASSESSED. Your learner should always know the rules of your course. Otherwise, it'll be difficult for them to play along. If you incorporate assessment tools that have consequences for your learner, such as a threshold for correct answers on a quiz or a pass rate for the course, you should communicate that clearly to them.

The Main Course Content

In order to create the main content for your course, you'll want to bring back your notes from the *what, why,* and *how* process. Remember that the *what, why,* and *how* process helped you to create a course structure? Creating the content, however, you'll have to switch focus to your learner and twist your notes around from "*what, why, how*" to "*why, what, how.*"

Making this switch will help you to immediately present your learner with a goal they want to achieve—their why—so they'll be engaged and open to learning something new. The goal will catch their attention. Without this goal in sight, your learner won't understand the purpose of the course and it will be much more likely they will not be engaged. The results? A low learning outcome. You have to inspire your learner.

Then comes the what. When you write your scripts to support the topics you want to teach—that's the what—the structure of your videos can vary, depending on how much you want to say about each topic. If you discover you've created a six-minute video, you might want to convert it into two videos of three minutes each.

Not every course will have a how, but if yours does, you'll incorporate that next.

Let's look at two examples of how you can divide your content into one or more videos, depending on how much content you have.

This first example applies when your content is fairly short:

- Video explaining why, what and how

Or

1. Video explaining why and what
2. Video explaining how

Now, HERE'S AN EXAMPLE FOR WHEN YOUR COURSE IS LONG, detailed, with a lot of content:

- Video explaining why
- Video explaining what
- Video explaining how

Structuring Your Scripts

When I create scripts, I usually create a document and insert a two-column table for each of the topics I have in my course. The first column contains my notes from the *what, why,* and *how* process (now written in the order *why, what,* and *how*) so I can easily see what my content has to include. Below that, in the second column, I write the script itself.

If I can see that a script is getting too long, I either try to shorten it or I choose to divide it into an additional video.

I've mentioned already that you want to write the body of your course content in such a way as to grab and hold your learner's attention. Here are some guidelines to help you do that.

Communicate the WHY

Communicating the *why* is about getting attention. This is also known as "the hook." Speak to the *learner's* interests, not the interest of the instructors. Include one or more of the following when writing your *why*:

- why the material is important to them
- what difference it will make to them or others (Pathos)
- present a problem or ask a question that the learner simply must learn the answer to
- include surprising statistics (Logos). For example: (a) how others have benefited from this knowledge, or (b) what research shows

This approach will help your learner understand *why* they should learn what you are about to teach them.

Communicate the WHAT

Communicating the *what* is about presenting the knowledge in a way they can understand. To do this, you will want to include one or more of the following when writing your *what*:

- relate to or build on prior learning/videos
- give examples/scenarios they can relate to (Pathos)
- highlight and compare things
- examine common mistakes and pitfalls
- incorporate analogies, even anecdotes
- use examples that directly relate to practice
- use arguments, facts, procedures, etc. (Logos)

An effective tool you can use in your *what* videos is to ask simple questions with a short pause after each to allow the learner to process. Then continue to talk after that break. It could look like this:

1. present some facts about the theory/approach/product
2. ask a question
3. insert a pause
4. answer the question for them after letting them consider their own answer

"So, we can say that knowing *x* can make a big difference for us. Would you like to know how you can do it yourself? (Two-second pause.) You can do it yourself by..."

Communicate the HOW

Many learners need to see *how* the knowledge can be applied in practice. Simply being told isn't effective for them. Depending on the nature of your content, there are different ways you can achieve this:

- filming a real-life situation, using the knowledge from the *what* part in practice
- an animation that illustrates a scenario where the *what* part is applied in practice
- using storytelling and telling a story about how the *what* part has been applied in practice
- an interview session/Q&A with a person that explains how he or she uses or has used the knowledge from the *what* part in practice

The Virtues of Brevity

A learner's receptivity is greatest during the first five minutes of a lecture. After ten minutes, it begins to decline dramatically. In an online context, it's even more crucial to be aware of the length of a lecture. In one of the largest studies of video engagement during MOOC sessions, researchers Philip Guo, Juho Kim, and Rob Rubin examined 6.9 million video watching sessions across the edX (Harvard & MIT) MOOC platform. These are some of their main findings:

- shorter videos are much more engaging
- informal talking-head videos are more engaging
- even high-quality pre-recorded classroom lectures might not make for engaging online videos

This research also showed that the best video length for an online learning session is about five minutes: the learner starts losing attention if the video is longer.

Content Creation without Video

Sometimes, it's just not possible to use video. In those instances, do what you can to work around it. Use any other technique available to you, provided it works with your context and content, and make sure you create the content following sound learning principles. In Section III: Apply, you'll find a case study from Lundbeck which includes an example of how I created course content without using video. While I always recommend video, I recognise that sometimes we need to move on without it.

17. Creating Educational Video

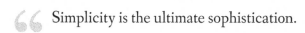

" Simplicity is the ultimate sophistication.

Leonardo Da Vinci

W hen your scripts are written, reviewed, and rehearsed, you're ready to record your videos.

Research shows that pedagogy is more important than technology. Let me tell you a story that explains the point:

In the 1970s, the famous Danish writer, Klaus Rifbjerg, said to a photographer, "The pictures you create are amazing! Delicious in the colours, sharp and dusty. Damn, you must have a great camera!"

The photographer replied, "It's a lot of fun. I'm glad you mentioned it, Klaus. I'm really crazy about your books. They fit well in the rack and I'm always looking forward to reading the next work from your hand. Such language, your characters, and the whole rhythm. Damn, you must have a good typewriter!"

The point of the story is that you don't have to invest in the most expensive cameras and software, although it's your privilege to do as you wish. Creating effective online learning courses and accompanying videos does not require the highest-class professional equipment.

If you have crisp video with excellent sound quality and a person talking rubbish on screen, learning outcomes will be low.

If you have someone presenting pedagogically-sound content in a video that has less-than-stellar picture and sound quality, learning outcomes will still be good.

If you don't have the resources to hire a professional to assist with your video production, you can still create video that produces a good learning outcome. Not being able to hire a professional is not a reason to forgo video and it should not stop you from creating your online learning course.

There are pedagogical and practical tips to apply whether you hire a professional video team or shoot the videos yourself. Following the tips I provide in *Achieving Change* will help you to create more engaging videos that increase learning outcomes.

Before you start recording, remember that your pedagogical learning design mindset gives you a different perspective than someone with a background in media production or feature film. Keep this in mind as you field advice from a professional media team, friends, colleagues, Google, or YouTube. You are creating *educational* videos, not just videos.

Pedagogical Tips

Authenticity is key. Consider what's authentic as you choose your settings, presenter location and style, and the case studies or examples you use in the video.

Real-life locations where the business or activity that's the focus of the training occurs are authentic settings. Authentic settings are often better choices than studios. To increase authenticity, it makes sense if people featured on camera are relaxed and in their regular, real settings. Trying too hard to place them in a fancy studio or clever setting can harm authenticity, diminish intimacy, and make it more difficult for the learner to connect and engage.

For interviews with other SMEs you wish to include in your video, I recommend you conduct the on-camera interview at their workplace, in their real-life setting. Remember the zookeeper interviewed in a zoo with animals behind him? Awesome. If your subject was computer programming, it would be authentic to film the presenter at their desk with the computer in view. In other words, keep it real.

Talk to the Learner

When you teach in a video, you have to ensure you are on the same level as the learner. Seeing the instructor's face has a powerful effect on engagement and credibility and provides an anchor for delivery of the information.

In other words, you don't want to be looking down, or up, to the camera. That camera lens represents the eye of your learner. Talk to the camera is essentially talking directly to the learner.

Don't explain or draw models (charts, graphs, and the like) if they make you look away from the learner or, even worse, if they make you turn your back to them. Instead, draw or print out the models in advance and present them to camera while you explain them to the learner, without showing your side or back to the camera.

Also, use real case studies or examples that have actually happened. It's better to tell true stories to show ideas, rather than resorting to, "Imagine this scenario." It will be more authentic and invoke Pathos.

Teleprompter

Here's what I've seen happen more times than I can count: The presenter tries to memorise the script. Tries, and fails, with many re-takes attempted. Once the presenter realises the memorisation approach isn't working, their next attempt usually involves holding notes with bullet points next to the camera. Then they discover two things: First, that it's obvious that they are not looking into the camera as they talk. Second, the paper makes too much rustling noise and destroys the audio quality. Eventually they change to the teleprompter and are impressed by how well it works.

I recommend using a teleprompter, and a teleprompter app, when recording videos, no matter if you use smartphones or professional cameras. A teleprompter will save you the hassle and energy of memorising a script. There won't be any difference between your script and what you say in the video. My experience is that a teleprompter will dramatically increase your usable material. If you film 100 minutes using a teleprompter, you can have up to ninety minutes of usable material but only five to ten minutes without one.

You don't have to buy a $4,000 teleprompter with a built-in screen. If you have an iPad or any other tablet, you can buy a quality teleprompter case (to fit over the camera) for as little as $200. Then download a teleprompter app. Some apps feature voice recognition, so you won't need somebody to scroll manually through your text.

One disadvantage in using a teleprompter is that it takes a bit of practice before a presenter will sound natural. However, with a little practice and help, almost anyone can effectively use a teleprompter. Here is some sage advice:

- talk naturally
- speak at a natural pace (not too slowly)
- allow pauses between sentences or questions so the learner has time to reflect
- smile more than you might normally (a lot)
- start and end a video with a big authentic smile

With respect to smiling, I'm not talking about big, fake, toothy grins. Find a way to enjoy yourself for real.

Even when using a teleprompter, it will still be tempting to try to memorise a script and work that way. This rarely works. I've tried to memorise scripts or work with clients who try to memorise many times. We always resort to the prompter.

Visuals

There is a concept in television journalism called "say dog, see dog." Any good journalist knows that if you're talking about a big yellow dog, then you show a picture of a big yellow dog. The reverse is also true—if you're showing a picture of a dog then you'd best be talking about a dog too.

One reason behind this concept is to constantly engage and entertain the brain of the viewer, otherwise it will switch off. Another reason is that the viewer/learner is unable to register both visuals and audio at the same time unless they are identical. If you show a quote on screen, you either have to read the quote aloud or give the learner time to read it before you address it. It's not possible for the human brain to read the quote and listen to your interpretation of it at the same time.

In an online learning context with videos, however, there are other reasons to use images and visuals to support your spoken word.

Using visuals such as highlighted text, facts, or figures can help you address logic (Logos). It will help your learner expend less mental energy trying to understand what you communicate, and it will also make it easier for them to recall later. When a learner hears *and* sees text, facts, or figures, it increases stimulated reflection, which helps them transfer the content from the short- to the long-term memory. For example, if you tell your learner there are three rules to follow, highlight key concepts from these rules as visuals. Or, if you make reference to numbers, percentages, currency amounts, show those on screen as you mention them.

Images and Pathos

There are going to be times when it's not possible to produce real-life case stories as moving video. Still images incorporated into your video can help you address Pathos (emotion) in your learner. This fosters an understanding of your content in less time and your learner will be able to remember it better. Think of a commercial from The Red Cross that aims to collect money to feed starving children. Pay attention to your emotional response when their spoken word is supported with images of emaciated or sick children. The pictures are triggering your Pathos and they will—whether or not you choose to donate—trigger your feelings and stick in your memory better than the spoken word alone.

When you use images in your videos, you can add a zoom or pan effect to make them more engaging. This will help to engage and entertain the learner's brain and promote maintained attention.

In addition to images and videos, animations are a great tool to include in your online learning videos. Often it's only possible to film videos explaining the *why* and *what* but not the *how*. Animations can assist you in this by helping illustrate scenarios that show your learner how to use the newly-learned knowledge in practice.

In one of the online courses I've created I had Frank Høedt (who provided illustrations for Achieving Change) to draw scenarios to support the spoken word of the instructor in the videos. I then observed five different learners as they watched the videos, and I looked for clues as to how the illustrations and animations affected their attention. In all five cases, the learners engaged with the video and they maintained their attention to the end. I then asked the learners what they felt was good and bad about the videos. One the things they highlighted as being very positive was the drawings, reporting that they had helped them to better understand the content.

Both from science and my own practical experience it stands clear that images, drawings, and animations are an important tool for learning designers.

This will help you heighten learning outcomes as you make the *how* section less abstract. It will take less mental energy in understanding how to apply the new knowledge into their own practice and provide motivation for them to apply and learn from experience.

Step Four:
Create the Scripts

18. Technical Setup and Advice

> ❝ Don't let your ears hear 'video' and your mind automatically think 'Hollywood budget.' Daring to think differently can help take your next e-learning course to a new level of learning engagement – and that really is the goal, after all.

> Chris Van Wingerden, dominKnow Learning Systems

I f you choose to do the filming yourself, or your circumstances prevent you from hiring professional production support, there are some technical tips that will help you create much more effective videos. Even if you are hiring help, this bit of technical advice will help you speak the same language as your producer.

Before You Begin

You might have an app on your smartphone which will provide limited ability to record, edit, or otherwise manipulate the content you create. Or, you might have video editing software on your

106

computer. There are several options, all with different capabilities and features. It's possible to create effective video materials for online learning using just a smartphone, provided you have the skills to produce quality. If you don't already have an app or software, the information that follows will help you understand what level of functionality you need.

Be conscious of the length of videos and of individual scenes or segments within. Remember that during a speech or lecture, learner's receptivity is greatest during the first five minutes. It begins to decline dramatically after ten. In an online context, it's even more crucial to be aware of length. Keep it as short as you can while still conveying the necessary information.

You want to have your scripts completely written, reviewed, and rehearsed before recording a single second of audio or video. Prepare the scripts according to the pedagogically-sound learning principles and steps outlined so far in *Achieving Change*.

Technical Setup

I use three different setups when I film, depending on the situation and the budget.

SETUP ONE: two professional cameras, with professional lights, and professional clip-on microphones.

SETUP TWO: two smartphones, one with a quality microphone attached.

SETUP THREE: one smartphone equipped with a microphone.

There are good reasons for using two cameras or two smartphones:

1. If you make a mistake while filming, you can easily go back one sentence and start again at that point without having to reshoot the entire video. When you edit, you can cut between the two camera angles, so learners won't notice your mistake.

2. Switching between camera angles every five to ten seconds will enliven the content and make it more engaging.

. . .

Sound

Good quality sound could make or break your video. Don't worry though. It's not as hard as you might think. Here are a few things to pay attention to:

1. The room. Record your video (and audio) in a room that's not too large. If the room has furniture and angled walls, all the better. This helps to minimise the sound reflection and will give your narrator's voice a more intimate, warm sound and draw the listener in.

2. The microphone. Use an external microphone. The microphones on your smartphones or camera may be good enough quality, but speakers will be positioned farther away from the source of the audio (the narrator's voice) than if the microphone was detached from the camera or phone and placed close to the source. A lapel (clip-on) mic or traditional mic on a stand is best. Place the mic as close as you can to the narrator's mouth without it showing on camera.

3. The recording levels. Most of the newer microphones will have a small LED which shows when the signal is good (loud enough) or bad (too loud or low). If the mic has no indicator, the software or other systems you are using should have a recording level indicator that you can rely on. You don't want the level to be too loud, or too soft, you want it just right. I once filmed a video session myself with some new equipment, where I forgot to look after the audio level. Too late I found out that the volume was set too loud and I had to re-do the entire film session. After that experience I always do several test shoots to ensure the sound level is right before I do the

actual filming. It's better to test one time too many than one time too little.

Common Mistakes

- Trying to memorise the script and wasting time before finally choosing the teleprompter.
- Forgetting to test the audio before filming.
- Having too much space above the head of the presenter. Don't cut the head off, but leave only about one centimetre of space above the head.
- Forgetting to shoot at an angle that allows you to add text or images beside the instructor in the editing process.
- Adding text on screen that's different from what the speaker is saying. The human mind can't both read and listen if it's not 100 per cent identical. If you add text, you'll have to read it out loud to speak directly to it.
- Not being aware of reflections of the camera or other objects if filming against a window or a shiny surface.

Step Four:
Create the Scripts

Step Four Review

Apply Your New Knowledge

- How can you use Ethos to support the SME and influence your learner?
- What examples, anecdotes or case studies can you use to make the content emotionally appealing to students?
- What facts, examples, precedents, authority, or deductive/inductive reasoning will help support your points?
- Review video of yourself and/or your SME and check the body language. Do you notice gestures, expressions, or movements that you didn't realise you were doing? Is there anything to change?
- Have you written your script before you pick up a camera? This will ensure you're clear about what to say and how to say it. Write the script after you design the course. Essentially, the script will be a result of the online learning design and thus, it will reflect how well you did

your job as a learning designer. We need to put the cart before the horse. Good content and design are the cart, the script and video production are the horse.

- Have you structured the course with information about the instructor, content material, and how to use the material—in that order? As you build your course, ensure that you follow this order.
- Did you apply all the principles and recommendations in steps one through four? Where are your weak areas? Where are your strong areas? Check your work prior to implementing it. Once you think you are ready to start filming, go over your course content again.
- Knowing that you have a maximum of ten minutes before you start to lose your learner's attention, how can you ensure that you cover the most important points?

Achieving Change

Step One :
Know The Learning Brain

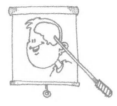

Step Five:
Assesment for Learning

Step Two:
Initiate Course Development

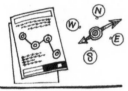

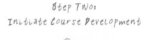

Step Four:
Create the Scripts

Step Three:
Engage the Learner

Step Five:
Assessment for Learning

19. Assessment Tools

> Most teachers waste their time by asking questions that are intended to discover what a pupil does not know, whereas the true art of questioning is to discover what the pupil does know or is capable of knowing.
>
> Albert Einstein

Once you have created your engaging content, your next task is to guide your learner through the content and to help them remember it. You want your learner to achieve the learning goals you have set for the course. And you want them to feel a sense of achievement, see real results and real value through their participation in your course.

Whether you are selling a course to customers or creating a course for internal use in an organisation, your benchmark for success should be how well you have helped the learner achieve the learning goals.

There are four main types of assessment tools you can use for learning purposes:

1. Multiple choice
2. Polls
3. Peer instruction
4. Peer assessment

Multiple Choice

During my bachelor studies at the Danish School of Education (DPU), almost all the professors condemned multiple choice assessment. I never understood why, but during my exchange in Portugal, it became clear.

While studying in Portugal, I enrolled in a course at the university about distance learning. The lecturer was in Lisbon, far away from where I studied in Faro, so I never personally met with him. He sent me a PDF version of the book *The Theory and Practice of Online Learning* by Terry Anderson (the book that got me interested in online learning) with instructions to read it carefully. At the end of the semester was an exam.

In Denmark, the tradition is for oral exams, so I was surprised that my final exam only consisted of a multiple-choice test. I had never before completed a course where the assessment consisted solely of multiple-choice questions. I remember that I was summoned to an old office where a professor sat at a desk in front. He handed me a bunch of papers turned face down. He then set a timer for one hour and instructed me to turn the papers over. No books, computer, or other items were allowed. All I had was a pencil, which the professor duly replaced with a pen. It was clear that I didn't know the rules.

As I read the multiple-choice questions, I was surprised that passing the course relied on my ability to *remember* facts from the book—not on my ability to *use* and *apply* the actual knowledge. I had difficulties with some of the questions. Depending on which perspective I adopted to view the questions, there was often more than one possible correct option. At university in Denmark, I was taught to think critically and was assessed on the way I combined knowledge and theory and then applied them to solve cases. But in this course in Portugal, I was assessed solely on my ability to remember details from a book.

After returning to Denmark and starting on my master's degree, my interest in multiple choice as an assessment tool grew and I started to experiment with it. My multiple-choice experience in Portugal raised the question of the value of testing recall of taught content, where each learner has a few answer options with one or more of them being correct. I wondered whether multiple choice could be used in a smarter way. Could it be used to test skills, rather than memorised knowledge?

After hours of reading theory and scientific articles about multiple choice, and testing it in different ways, I determined that multiple choice is an assessment tool that has been misused for many years, and that—if used the right way—holds great potential. I created a new approach to creating multiple choice questions that has made it possible to test skills as well as knowledge. It's now also possible to guide the learner in achieving their desired learning outcome. I'll describe how you can create effective multiple-choice quizzes in the next chapter.

Polls

One of the elements that traditional e-learning lacks when compared to face-to-face learning is involving learners and establishing communication between them. Thus, many online course providers struggle with high dropout rates. Disciplined learners manage to complete online courses, but less disciplined learners need help feeling engaged in the course. They need to feel they are not alone. One way to engage learners in your course is through polls. Research from McKinsey Academy shows that polls can help to "foster more engagement as users' sense connections with other members of the cohort." In the specific McKinsey Academy course, the completion rate was above 90 per cent.

Presenting learners with a poll triggers their curiosity about what other people think about the content or topic. As well, knowing their answers in the poll will count in the shared results, learners will put more effort into their contribution to the poll, think carefully before they provide an answer to the poll, and be motivated to learn the content before they submit their answer.

Polls help the learner engage in the course and to think critically about the content in the course, as they are able to see his or her own contribution, as well as comparing it with the other learners in the course. This makes them aware of a different way to view the new information, which prompts them to review how they reached their initial conclusion and reassess. Suddenly, the contribution to the poll counts, as other learners will be able to see the contribution, and on top of that, each learner feels part of a learner community rather than participating on their own.

Polls for Improving Your Course

Another effective use of polls is as a tool for you as learning designer to continually improve your course offering by giving each learner a voice. Polls, after each module or after the course, asking the learner to apply a rating, e.g. between one and five stars, and then explain the reason for their rating, provide valuable information about their perspective and experience. How better to keep the learner in mind than to ask them directly to share what's in their mind? You could ask how they liked a new feature, whether there is anything else they'd like to see included in the course, and whether the course content added value to their work.

Poor ratings and feedback allow you to see what isn't working and adjust. Positive ratings and feedback tell you what you can do more of. Using polls this way helps you develop courses with content that learners actively seek and that address their learning preferences. As well, by asking learners to contribute, you are giving them a voice. They will likely feel a sense of ownership and of being part of something bigger. They're not simply participants; they're co-creators helping improve the course for future learners.

Peer Instruction

Peer instruction is a social assessment tool that's part of a new generation of multiple choice—with a social dimension. By adding a social element, it's possible for the learner to add and share an explanation about their choice in the quiz. And on top of that, the learner is able to see other learners' explanations, which means two things:

1. They know other learners will see their contribution, so they're motivated to think critically and put an effort into their explanation.
2. They learn from one another and get insights into the experiences of others, which helps them see things from new perspectives and revise their opinions. This is a huge step forward for online learning as it enhances the change-oriented experience for learners.

Although the peer instruction social assessment tool is not part of every learning management system (LMS), it can bring inspiration to any learning designer. I encourage you to add the concept to your assessment mindset and think creatively about how to use multiple choice.

Here's how peer instruction works in practice:[1]

1. Explain your choice
2. Review other initial responses
3. Revise your response
4. Review the correct answer
5. Compare answers

1. Explain Your Choice

The learner is presented with a question, as in traditional multiple choice, and they must choose an answer. In addition, they are prompted to explain why they chose each answer to the multiple-choice questions.

This step is an opportunity to provide a persuasive argument about why the answer is the correct one. The answer might include references to a course video, or a practical experience, or a description of how the learner arrived at their choice.

The answer that the learner chose, together with this explanation, comprises their initial response. When the learner selects *next*, their initial response is added to the collection of initial responses by all of the other course participants.

2. Review Other Initial Responses

The learner then reviews the initial responses submitted by other course participants. As the learning designer, you decide how many other responses the learner will see: they might see one response for each of the possible answer choices, or a set that's chosen at random from the collection in step one.

This step gives the participant a chance to learn from the explanations that other learners submitted, and to reassess their own understanding of the topic.

3. Revise Your Response

The learner can now decide whether he/she wants to change the initial response by selecting a different answer choice, revising their explanation, or both.

This is an optional step. The learner can submit a final response and explanation that are the same as their initial response, or they can change their answer completely. If the learner chooses to change or add details to their explanation, the updated explanation will substitute their explanation in the collection from number one above, *Explain Your Choice.*

When they move on to the next step, they learn the correct answer.

4. REVIEW THE CORRECT ANSWER

The learner can now review the correct answer choice and the explanation provided by the learning designer.

5. COMPARE ANSWERS

In the last step, if you're using an LMS with the peer instruction social assessment tool, the learner will see shared graphs that reveal the percentage of learners who selected each answer. The first graph shows the percentage of learners who selected each answer initially, and the second graph shows the percentage of learners who selected each answer after they had the opportunity to review the explanations that other learners provided. The learners can compare their own choices, and the correct one, to the answers from their peers. (The graphs appear only after ten learners submit their final responses.)

Peer Assessment

In my view, peer assessment is the most useful assessment method in online learning, both for learning and measuring. You can use peer assessment to support the basic conditions needed to facilitate transformative learning for your learners, including the development of critical thinking and changes in opinions and attitude, as we discussed in Step One: Know the Learning Brain. You can also use it to measure the higher-cognition-level analysis, synthesis, and evaluation.

Peer assessment is powerful because it facilitates social learning and allows the learner to answer questions openly, share experiences, and explain their opinions to other learners.

Peer assessment is different from teacher-to-participant assessment, such as multiple choice, where the teacher, often in a position of authority, either assesses or guides the participant. Instead, peer assessment is participant-to-participant. Peers on the same level offer personal feedback to assess and guide each other. Studies show that peer feedback has "greater immediacy than teacher feedback and that a peer assessor with less skill at assessment but more time in which to do it can produce an assessment of equal reliability and validity to that of a teacher."[2] Some studies even find peer feedback to be more encouraging, forward-looking, offering more concrete help than teacher feedback.[3]

HERE'S HOW PEER ASSESSMENT WORKS:

1. The instructor asks an open question.
2. Participants submit their answer individually to the question. The answer can be text, video, or image.
3. The learning management system automatically divides participants into groups. The participants within a group are presented with the answers from the other group members and based on assessment guidelines prepared by the learning designer, they grade the other participants' answers and give personalised feedback that explains the grade.
4. Each participant receives the grades and the explanation of the grades from the other participants in the group.

You can use peer assessment in many ways and to achieve many different learning outcomes. You can direct the focus of the peer assessment activities to highlight how the learner applied new theory while working on the job. Or it could also be the learner showing a product or a plan they've developed and getting feedback from peers.

Because peer assessment allows the learner with opportunity to explain their answer, it's possible to use it to assess informal learning (learning from practice or learning outside the curriculum).

20. Effective Assessment

" When students learn through student-centric online technology, testing doesn't have to be postponed until the end of an instructional module and then administered in a batch mode. Rather, we can verify mastery continually to create tight, closed feedback loops.

Clayton Christensen, Harvard Business School

Assessment is how you can guide the learner to achieve the learning goals, create long-lasting learning, learn new skills, and develop competencies that help them improve their on-the-job behaviour.

I'm not referring to traditional assessment. That's "teaching for the test," where instructors test only whether the learner can remember what they have been told.

No matter what assessment tools or options you have available, effective assessment means keeping the learner in mind. It means understanding that assessment should be used:

- to guide the learner, so they know whether they are on the right track
- as a means to move experience and knowledge from short-term to long-term memory
- to foster on-the-job behaviour change
- to encourage and assess higher-order and critical thinking skills

To create what I call "assessment for learning," I'll introduce the concepts that set the strategic baseline for effective assessment. I'll also show you how to create multiple-choice questions that promote learning.

In order to get results from using assessment tools such as multiple choice, polls, peer instruction, and peer assessment, you have to have an assessment mindset. Using the tools without this mindset is like flying a plane without taking any pilot training. You might manage to start the plane and even get it off the ground, but the entire flight will be a terrible experience for your passengers. Assessment tools on their own won't lead to change or skill or competency development. They're just tools. If not used the right way, they won't have any value. You need an assessment mindset in order to pilot the learning plane.

Learner-Centred Assessments

A common mistake among instructors is creating assessment elements that test rote learning. Memory alone isn't enough. You want to guide the learner to reflect and acquire useful skills.

To create assessment that guides each learner, you have to think about the assessment from your learner's perspective. Better yet, think of yourself *as a learner* going through your course.

Reflection

The concept of reflection is key in the questions you create for your assessment tools. I've seen far too many SMEs create questions that don't incorporate reflection, and as a result they don't prompt any learning.

You need to build your own knowledge of reflection into your assessment mindset if you want to achieve high learning outcomes for your learner and assess their skills (analyse and apply) and competencies (evaluate and create).

Contemporary research in neuropedagogy (aka learning and the brain) shows that reflection is one of the keys to move impressions from the short- to long-term memory and create a long-lasting learning outcome. Furthermore, reflection can help the learner to put aside old habits and be open to learning new things and willing to change.

There are two types of reflection: regular reflection and critical reflection.

Regular reflection is what helps the learner move the newly learned knowledge into the long-term memory. It takes place when the learner looks back over new knowledge or experiences of how to approach a challenge, which can be connected to assimilative and accommodative learning.

Critical reflection is a deeper level of reflection that facilitates transformative learning and prompts the learner to change opinions, attitudes, and habits. It takes place when the learner looks back at the premise or basis for a challenge and thereby starts to consider why they should be open to changing his/her opinions, attitudes and habits.

The questions you want to create to facilitate reflection for your learner – both regular and critical reflection – can be divided into three levels:

1. *what* questions (reflection over content)

2. *how* questions (reflection over the process)
3. *why* questions (reflection over the premise for one's opinions, attitudes, and habits)

What and *how* questions lead to regular reflection while *why* questions lead to critical reflection. While you can facilitate regular reflection using polls and multiple choice, it's only possible to facilitate critical reflection through peer assessment.

Creating Your Own Questions

You'll recall that the brain contains hundreds of mental boxes, each of which holds knowledge and understanding within a specific area.

When we learn, we can add new content to the boxes (assimilative learning), change the current content of the boxes (accommodative learning) or break down and reconstruct the boxes and change their interconnectivity (transformative learning).

New knowledge gets stored in these mental boxes through one of six types of learning categories. Which learning category is best for your reflection-type assessment questions will be dictated by your learning goals. And together, these will tell you what questions you need to create for your assessments.[1]

- INSTRUMENTAL LEARNING involves predictions about events that can be observed. After testing the theory or tool, the prediction may turn out to be correct or incorrect. *What are the facts? How do I know this is true? Why is this knowledge important to me?*

- COMMUNICATIVE LEARNING involves learning through dialogue, reaching an understanding of other learners' assumptions, beliefs, and perspectives, and discovering and articulating their own. *What do others say about this?*

How did I integrate others' points of view? Why should I believe in my conclusion?

- EMANCIPATORY LEARNING is a cognitive process whereby the learner considers the reasons for their assumptions, beliefs, and perspectives, how they arrived at them, and why they should revise or retain these assumptions. *What are my assumptions about this? How do I know my assumptions make sense? Why should I revise or retain my perspective?*

- THE EPISTEMIC is the learner's self-awareness of their knowledge, assumptions, beliefs, and perspectives. *What do I believe about myself? How have I come to this perception of myself? Why should I question this perception?*

- THE SOCIOLINGUISTIC is about the social norms, cultural habits, and ideologies that motivate the learner and their learning preferences. *What are the social norms? How have the social norms been influential? Why are these norms important?*

- THE PSYCHOLOGICAL is what the learner believes about themselves, how they've come to this belief, and why they should question their self-perception (theories, directions, self-understanding, personality traits). *What knowledge do I have? How did I obtain this knowledge? Why do I need or not need this knowledge?*

YOU'LL SEE EXAMPLES OF HOW I CREATED QUESTIONS IN THE Henley Business School and Fairstart case study examples found in Section III: Apply.

Summative and Formative Assessment

Summative assessment, which is the most common type of assessment, looks backward. It tests if a learner can remember what they've been taught. The most common use of summative assessment is the multiple-choice quiz, using content from the course. Learners are awarded points for correctly remembering content. If they achieve enough points, or correct answers, they pass. If not, they fail.

The purpose of formative assessment, on the other hand, is to guide the learner and promote more effective learning. Formative assessment is most commonly implemented in the off-line learning context, for example, a learner presenting their work and receiving personal feedback from an instructor. Watch for ways to integrate formative assessment in addition to summative assessment when you design your course. This can include writing an explanation with the answers to your multiple-choice quizzes (we will look into this in a moment), so the learner will know why he or she is wrong if submitting an incorrect answer. Or it can be peer feedback in peer assessment, with deep personalised feedback. Bottom line is that from the learner's perspective, formative assessment helps them to identify their strengths and weaknesses and target areas they need to improve. And from your point of view as a learning designer, it helps you to recognise where your learner is struggling. You can address problems immediately or improve content in specific areas.

Ongoing Assessment

What do you do when you know that there's a final assessment, or test, at the end of any course you've taken? You're just like the rest of us who will put in a huge effort to memorise the content just to pass the test.

If you only provide assessments at the end of a course, you risk having misunderstandings that persist for hours, days, or even weeks, until the exam takes place. At that point, when the learner discovers this misunderstanding, it's too late to correct. Shouldn't the learner have the opportunity to correct their misunderstandings immediately? To adjust, to learn, and to incorporate the intended learning into their behaviour? I say yes.

Imagine these two scenarios.

SCENARIO ONE: you are participating in a course that takes five days to complete. At the end of day five you are presented with a final assessment with fifty multiple choice quiz questions in random order. You get thirty-five of the questions right and fifteen wrong. You look at the fifteen wrong answers and wonder to which part of the course each of them relates. With all the content that you have been through the past five days it's almost impossible to remember. And you aren't likely to have a chance to find out.

SCENARIO TWO: you are participating in the same five-day course, but after each video and each major topic you have to answer a few questions that relate to the content. You immediately discover whether you have understood the content. And you have the opportunity to re-watch the videos or re-read the material to correct your misunderstanding.

You want to design your course so that your learner experiences the second scenario. It will help you guide each learner. It's more engaging and less stressful. And it also provides opportunities for your learner to continuously reflect and thereby move the new knowledge from short- to long-term memory.

It's such a simple concept and requires only a small change when you create your courses. However, the impact it will have is significant. You can also use this kind of assessment to track the effectiveness of your course content. Typically, a group of learners will produce varied responses to the questions in an assessment. If every learner provides correct or incorrect answers, you know that something may be wrong with either the quiz or the video, and you will have an opportunity to adjust the course content.

Situational Assessment

Most instructional designers create assessment the traditional way: providing content and assessing the learner's ability to remember the content. But what good is remembering facts and concepts if you are not able to use them in real life? The sole learning outcome will be an ability to recite the memorised knowledge but not much else. But what if there was a way to assess each learner's ability to act and remember, rather than only remembering? There is such a way, and that's the situational assessment.

The concept of situational assessment is about linking content to a practical situation, and about assessing the learner's ability to apply the content in the situation. You will want to create a narrative that illustrates a practical situation or challenge that's plausible for your learner to face on their job and create questions that connect the course content to that scenario.

If your learner can imagine themselves in the situation described, they'll be more engaged in the assessment. It will help them understand the situation and reflect about how they would react. This reflection will help them connect the content to that practical application, and thereby they will learn how to *use* the knowledge when they face a real-life situation.

From your point of view as a learning designer, you'll not only assess your learner's knowledge, but also their ability to link the content to practice.

Situational assessment can be illustrated using a narrative. You can communicate the narrative through video or text, or an image supported by text.

Explaining Feedback

Imagine you are discussing something with a colleague. You express your understanding of the topic, and your colleague tells you that you are wrong. You would also expect your colleague to explain *why* you are wrong. And you would likely have a further discussion where your colleague would explain his viewpoint to you, and help you correct your understanding (if you agree with his arguments, of course).

Contrast this with traditional e-learning where a learner answers questions, one after the other, not knowing whether they are right or wrong until the test is complete, and marks are assessed. The discussion stops with, "You're wrong." They receive no guidance or feedback on why they were wrong or how to come to a better understanding.

To avoid misunderstandings and to guide the learner, explain your feedback. Explaining feedback is about giving an explanation to the learner immediately after answering a question in a quiz. If a learner provides an incorrect answer, you can tell the learner why the answer is wrong, along with what the correct answer is or what content to revisit to correct the misunderstanding. Explaining feedback also works when the learner provides a correct answer. You can also explain why the answer is correct, as it will confirm them in their understanding.

Second Attempt

Imagine you've discovered that you answered an assessment question incorrectly. Your heart sinks as you see your potential marks plummeting to the floor. Now imagine that you actually get a second attempt at answering this question. Feels good, right? Here's how it would work. First, you will have received the explanatory feedback. Then, you get a chance to go back and answer the question again. Would that motivate you to revise your first answer in order to get it correct? The answer will in most cases be a yes. To encourage your learner to correct their misunderstandings, in essence to truly learn the material, you will want to include a second attempt into the pass rate of your assessment. This could involve providing your learner with half as many points as you'd award if they had answered correctly on the first attempt.

Let's say you have ten questions and each question is worth ten points. To pass, your learner will need at least seventy points, which would mean answering seven of ten questions correctly. Using a second attempt, you would allow your learner to correct their misunderstandings on up to six of the questions, and still pass. This will encourage them to re-study the content as they get a reward for correcting their misunderstanding. That said, I don't recommend setting pass rates. Instead I advocate for the use of elements from gamification (game play), such as rules of play, point scoring, and competition with others. You can give each learner a title, and if possible, a badge, depending on the score. Instead of just passing, they will see a competition in becoming a part of a certain group.

For instance:

0-49 points: rookie

51-69 points: pro

70-100 points: champion

Writing Multiple Choice Quizzes

Learning designers often skip quickly over the process of writing multiple choice quizzes, without putting in much thought or effort because they don't believe it's a science. However, it is a science. The result of thinking it's easy to write multiple choice assessments and that anybody can do it is that the learner is left struggling and confused. You'll end up neither testing nor guiding your learner to a better learning outcome. I experienced this myself in Portugal. I've seen it at every single company I've worked with.

Here are some tips on how to write effective questions and possible answers.

Writing the Question

1. Choose the learning goal to be assessed and whether it's knowledge or skills.
2. Keep each quiz, test, and question distinct from any other: the learner shouldn't be able to provide the same answer for more than one question.
3. Keep the questions clear, concise, and understandable. The learner should spend time solving the problem rather than understanding what the problem is about.
4. Qualify the questions. For example, an unqualified question would be, *"What is the best comedy movie ever made?"* Whereas a qualified question would be, *"According to the Danish Film Institute, what's the best Danish comedy ever made?"*
5. Don't include trick questions.
6. Write your questions with a level of complexity suitable for your learner. Often including a short narrative is helpful.
7. Write the central idea or view into the question and not into the answers.
8. Avoid negative language: no, not, and except. If you must include these words, be sure to capitalise, underline, or select boldface font (NO, <u>not</u>, **except**).[2]

Answers

1. Watch that you're making each possible answer a similar length. Learning designers tend to make the correct answer longer than the rest.
2. All potential answers should be equally plausible.

3. You don't need to include more than three possible answers.
4. Of your possible answers, ensure only one is correct.
5. Mix up the placements of the correct answer, e.g., don't put all correct answers as the second, or all the third. Mix them up.
6. Avoid including response options such as *"None of the above,"* *"All of the above,"* and *"Do not know."*
7. Write incorrect answer choices that reflect typical errors.

Step Five:
Assessment for Learning

Step Five Review

Apply Your New Knowledge

- How can you incorporate formative assessments throughout your course and include summative assessments near the end? Can you combine the two throughout? The answer will depend on the assignments you choose and the structure of your course.
- How can your quizzes and multiple-choice tests inspire the learner to reflect?
- How might you incorporate peer assessments for each assignment you create?
- How can you get the learner thinking about and applying the content, in addition to quizzes, multiple-choice tests, and peer assessments?
- Consider the learning goals: what outcomes do you want from your course? How can you measure those outcomes?

Section III: Apply

CASE STUDIES !

21. The Fairstart Foundation Project

You'll recall that the Fairstart Foundation project involved developing an online learning programme that could be implemented across eighteen countries to train orphanage caregivers, with varying education levels and cultural backgrounds, on a consistent set of principles related to how to treat the children in their care. The training programme was designed to address these differing cultures, expectations, and beliefs around the handling, for example, of a crying child.

We focused our online learning programme on engaging the care-givers to apply the new knowledge right away in their workplace, and we provided a structured reflection approach to reinforce the benefits of the newly acquired skills. And as you'll soon see, the programme has had a direct impact on the happiness of the orphaned children in care.

In the case example that follows, I'll highlight particular segments of the process and the approach my co-founder Jeppe and I took in developing the programme.

Fairstart's 70/20/10

After doing a *what*, *why*, and *how* process with employees working at the orphanages at Fairstart, we agreed to structure the course considering the 70/20/10 approach (10/70/20 at Fairstart) in the following way:

- At the start of each week, learners would watch videos that presented theory and tools. We used problem-based learning by relating the theory to a problem to make it more tangible. (The 10 per cent.)
- We converted the theory into exercises and tools the learners would apply at the orphanages where they worked, thus getting real-life experience. (The 70 per cent.)
- At the end of each week, we then asked the learners to discuss and reflect upon their on-the-job experiences, giving and receiving feedback to and from their peers. (The 20 per cent.)

FAIRSTART 10 PER CENT

- Course overview
- Importance of understanding the theory behind caregiving
- How the theory could empower them on the job
- Interviews with children and caregivers explaining what difference the Fairstart physical training programmes have had for them
- A problem presented for solving
- Theory presentation
- Examples of the theory applied in practice
- Real-life observations
- Animations

FAIRSTART 70 PER CENT

- Application of theory by using the tools provided and getting real-life experience at the orphanages

FAIRSTART 20 PER CENT

- Online group-work assignments
- Learners submitted answers to questions that stimulated regular reflection and critical reflection.
- Learners reflected about what happened when they applied the theory, how it happened, and why it was important for them to know the theory. Each learner gave and received peer feedback to/from two other learners.

Problem-Based

The caregivers accessing the Fairstart online learning courses were exposed to real-world scenarios to support and reinforce their learning. This is the problem-based approach, the first of the five principles for creating engaging content.

Here's how we incorporated the problem-based principle.

1. *Problem*: we showed a video that explained that many caregivers have challenges with young children crying, particularly when children play on their own while caregivers have lunch.
2. *Theory*: it's beneficial to remain close to children who are playing on their own, without playing with them. Just being next to them is helpful.
3. *Application*: we gave each learner an assignment to have one caregiver sit close to the playing children as they ate lunch and see if there was a difference in the children's

behaviour from times when they were not in the
children's presence.

4. *Assessment*: the caregiver explained what they did and
why it worked according to the theory. A further
assignment could have been to create a plan for how to
schedule lunch at the workplace and assign different
caregivers to take turns having lunch near the children.

Demonstration

Third in our list of five principles for creating engaging content is
demonstration. With Fairstart, we used animation with storytelling to
support the transfer of theory into practice. We did this by:

- presenting a problem
- showing the animated caricatures using the theory to
  solve the problem
- showing a change in the children (from crying to smiling)

Ethos, Pathos, Logos at Fairstart

We created the Fairstart course content keeping Ethos, Pathos, and
Logos in mind.

The professor introduced himself and his professional background (Ethos). He presented case studies and statistics (Logos). He
then showed video interviews with former orphanage children, now
adults, talking about what it meant to them to have proper caregivers
and staff. This gave real-life, human explanations for how application
of the theory actually made a difference (Pathos).

When I began to create the Fairstart education materials, I saw
an interview with a girl who spoke about what it was like to lose her
parents and end up at an orphanage. Seeing and hearing the girl's
personal story helped motivate me and deepen my understanding
about the importance of the course. And I knew it would also moti-

vate the learners. This is an example of using Pathos: where the content addresses credibility, trustworthiness, reliability, and competence. Seeing the girl talking about her experience was credible. We trusted what she was telling us, and we could rely on the impact that the experience had on her life. It was much different from just reading facts about how many orphaned children get caught up in drug abuse, prostitution, or commit suicide due to ineffective caregiving.

We used the interview as a tool in the course. We shared an interview with another girl talking about her experience when a tsunami hit Sumatra. She talked about her entire family dying, leaving her all alone, and she shared what it meant to come to a place where she could have food and shelter. The girl starts to cry during the interview, which draws on the empathy of the learner, making them want to learn so they can help other parentless children.

Peer Assessment at Fairstart

We used the 70/20/10 approach as a starting point for developing the peer assessment.

Because the participants needed to participate in the peer assessment, to use the learned theory on the job, and to share experiences with peers about that on-the-job application, they were motivated to pay attention to the course content and the practical experience they then shared with their peers.

Social learning was critical for the Fairstart project. Because the caregivers were situated in multiple locations in eighteen countries, providing them with the means of engaging in peer assessment was central to their learning experience.

I used video to describe peer assessment, what it is and how it works, as well as the purpose and how and why it may seem like a foreign learning activity for the learners.

We ended each week of online learning modules with peer assessment. Learners were asked to think about, describe, and discuss with their peers how they converted the theory and information from the previous week into practice as they cared for the orphaned children.

Between sessions two and three the caregivers were asked to perform different tasks in their workplace, and to observe, use video, or write notes about things like:

- How the children reacted when the caregivers left them alone.
- How children responded when one caregiver acted as a secure base.
- Observing differences between how children respond when a caregiver leaves (some may cling or cry, other children may not notice but keep doing what they do, etc.).

Here is some of the actual text we used to guide the learners through the reflection and learning process.

WE WOULD LIKE YOU TO SHARE YOUR EXPERIENCES AND YOUR *thoughts about the caregivers' work and children's reactions based on session two.*

- *What tasks and activities did the caregivers perform between session two and three?*
- *How did the children react to the new ways of doing things?*
- *Why do you think the children's behaviour changed/didn't change when the caregivers tried the new activities?*

Peer feedback:
Please provide feedback to your fellow instructor and their interac-

tion with the caregiver group and if you believe he or she is on the right track. We would like you to rate their feedback as well as give an explanation to your rating that can help the instructor to know why you have rated as you have. Write at least three lines.

- *Very much on the right track (the instructor is creating a trustful and open learning environment)*
- *Much (the instructor is working to create the learning environment)*
- *Not much (the instructor is not discussing openly with the caregivers about the challenges there might be in group cooperation)*

After giving feedback to the instructors, we would now like you to provide an overall feedback. You should write at least ten lines. Please include an answer to the following questions in your feedback:

- *What do you believe is the most important in the instructor's feedback?*
- *Did you have similar or different experiences?*
- *Which development areas do you believe the instructor should work on in the future, and why should he or she do it?*

IN POST-PROGRAMME POLLS AND FEEDBACK QUESTIONNAIRES, all participants reported that peer assessment was a key part of their certification at the end of the training programme.

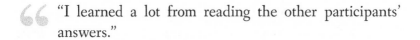 "I learned a lot from reading the other participants' answers."

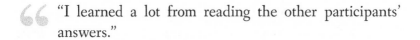 "I have learned so much! Not only about training

caregivers, but also about intercultural cooperation and about myself and my role as an instructor."

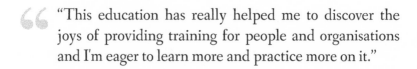 "This education has really helped me to discover the joys of providing training for people and organisations and I'm eager to learn more and practice more on it."

Fairstart Online Learning Results

The results from the online learning sessions at Fairstart show that 660 children in their care facilities were performing 20 per cent better than before our new online learning rolled out across the globe.

Now, caregivers respond at once to a child who cries or needs attention. They also show a vast change in mindset in that they understand the value of listening to and hearing the views of children. They say that it's a priority for them to allow the children to talk and find out what they think, feel, and want. This was a major difference in their mindsets from the onset of the training.

There were many other positive outcomes of the training:

- Children's overall well-being has improved.
- Relations between caregivers and children has improved.
- Caregivers have more satisfaction and pride in their jobs.
- Attachment theory translates into practice.
- Common care standards and methods are now in place. Instead of everybody doing their own thing, they now have standards and methods for doing their jobs. It's more structured and unified.

Caregivers reported paying more attention to children with different behavioural patterns. They took part in the children's lives, sports, and school activities. They spent more time with them. They tried to recognise the models/patterns of attachment in the children and act as the safe adult in the children's lives.

When asked to report on the response from the children, the caregivers reported that older ones seemed at first to be confused by the new ways of doing things. However, the children also expressed thankfulness and acceptance when they realised that caregivers paid more attention to them. Younger ones appeared to feel safer spending time in closer relationships with caregivers. The caregivers shared how one particular child who never smiled had been smiling since her caregiver started implementing secure attachment dimensions of care with her.

Several years after creating this online caregiver education, Jeppe and I continue to act as consultants for Fairstart, helping them keep their learning programmes up to date and to expand their online caregiver education to more countries and orphanages around the world. That is achieving change.

22. BESTSELLER

I have had the good fortune to work closely with the Danish retail clothing company, BESTSELLER, for a few years. (I'm not yelling. They present their brand name in all caps and I'm honouring them by doing the same.) In creating several online learning courses with them I have changed the way they design, develop, and deliver their training.

I'll be talking about elements of two courses I designed for BEST-SELLER throughout this case discussion: one related to consumer experience, another based on building product knowledge of the sales staff.

Consumer Experience Course

The company wanted its consumers to feel proud, secure, and satisfied about wearing their clothing and about the experiences in their stores. They had conducted a lot of SCORM-based training (you'll remember SCORM as the shareable content object reference model from Chapter 3: A Model History) that included the words proud, secure, and satisfied. It was a strategy designed to help the employees remember and focus on how the company wanted its customers to feel.

Later, the employees took tests to see how well they remembered the content in the training. The employees could repeat the words but when they tried to say *how* to make their customers feel proud, secure, and satisfied, they had no idea.

Summative and Formative

Since the objective of the course was to help employees understand how to change their behaviour so that the customer would have a better experience, I incorporated a feedback mechanism into a demonstration by combining quizzes with videos:

- Video: An instructor explains content or a situation.
- A quiz pops up on the video, asking how the learner thinks the instructor will act in the situation. If using animation or a story, quiz asks how the character in the story will act.
- Video: The instructor shows how to do it correctly or the character in the animation/story acts in the right way.

The above example illustrates how the combination of summative and formative assessment helps learners stop and reflect on the content. They should then get feedback to help them correct any misunderstandings. Feedback is a great way to motivate learners to put theory into practice.

This course was pivotal in changing the BESTSELLER training programmes away from an information-dump method toward training programmes that included demonstrations of *how* the employees could help make customers feel proud, secure, and satisfied.

Employees had to use the new tools and information by applying them on the job. When they finished, customers really did feel proud, secure, and satisfied, and I could happily say the same for the employees.

Product Knowledge Course

When creating videos for the product knowledge course, rather than merely explaining the different products (which would be devoid of any Ethos, Pathos, or Logos), we presented:

- the trainer and his professional background (Ethos);
- surveys with statistics about the impact product knowledge can have on sales (Logos);
- interviews with consumers, explaining what difference it makes for them when staff members know about the products (Pathos);
- interviews with staff, explaining the difference product knowledge makes for their experiences with the consumers (Pathos).

To invoke pathos at BESTSELLER, we included an interview with a consumer explaining how important it is for him to have a salesperson that can guide him when he wants to buy clothes.

We also included an interview with a staff member explaining how training in product knowledge has had a positive impact on his sales and at the same time made the work day more fun.

DEMONSTRATION

The trainer presented a product and then highlighted its features and benefits. At the end of each video, the trainer explained how to communicate this knowledge to a consumer by giving examples. (Some BESTSELLER courses had a higher budget and more time. In those cases, we installed cameras in a store and filmed actual interactions between a trainer and a real customer.)

. . .

VIDEOS

Our videos also contained information that made the learners aware that consumers want a knowledgeable salesperson. I introduced facts and numbers, then shared interviews with consumers talking about the importance of speaking to a knowledgeable salesperson. I also let the learners know:

- why they should take part in the training
- what they would do in the training
- what they would be able to do after the training (learning goals)
- how they would know they had achieved the learning goals
- how they could apply the knowledge and tools from the course in real life
- what assessments would be used and how real-life experience would be a part of the assessment.

The team at BESTSELLER often used smartphones to shoot video inside retail stores. They set up additional lighting and placed external microphones on the relevant spokespeople. The resulting videos worked well and were sometimes more engaging for learners than filming inside BESTSELLER's training facility. (Remember authenticity!)

ASSESSMENT

An assessment example from this course looked like this:

A GUY ENTERS THE STORE. AS YOU CONNECT WITH HIM, HE TELLS you that he exercises a lot and would like a pair of jeans that will make him look smart but at the same time will be comfortable to wear. What fitting would you offer him?

1. *Loose fit*
2. *Regular fit*
3. *Anti-fit*

You'll recall that it's effective to have each learner explain their action. In this example, learners explain why they would recommend a particular fitting.

I would recommend the Anti-fit as it has a regular rise, loose thigh and a loose knee that will offer a lot of comfort, and a narrow leg opening that will look stylish.

By incorporating quiz-type questions with each multiple-choice question, we were able to stimulate the learner's reflection, thus deepening the learning.

Let's look at an example from a traditional assessment that presents the facts but doesn't allow learners to commit the information to memory based on a situational presentation.

CONTENT (WHAT): PROVIDING FACTS ABOUT DIFFERENT TYPES OF jeans.
Quiz:
What characterises skinny fit jeans?

1. *Low rise, skinny thigh, super skinny knee, super tight leg opening*
2. *Low rise, super thigh, super skinny knee, super tight leg opening*
3. *Low rise, skinny thigh, skinny knee, skinny leg opening (correct)*

Here, by comparison, is a situational assessment which does help the learner understand the *how*, and therefore will help them commit the information to memory.

CONTENT (WHAT AND HOW): PROVIDING FACTS ABOUT different types of jeans and examples of how to use the knowledge on the job.

Quiz:

A guy enters your store. He is tall and thin, and it seems like he is in his late forties. After making a connection with him, you have the following conversation:

You: I would like two minutes of your time just to make it easier for you. What would you think of that?

Consumer: I like things easy.

You: Me too! First of all. Let me ask you how you like your jeans to fit and to look?

Consumer: I like my jeans straight up and down. I will wear the jeans at the office, so they should not stand out too much, and they should work well accompanied by a classic Oxford shirt.

You: When you say you like your jeans straight up, what do you mean?

Consumer: Straight up for me is when the jeans are not too loose and not too tight.

What would you then tell this consumer?

1. *I think a Regular Fit would be appropriate for you. We have a model called Clark (correct).*
2. *I think a Loose Fit would be appropriate for you. We have a model called Boxy.*
3. *I think a Slim Fit would be appropriate for you. We have a model called Tim.*

Polls

In the BESTSELLER courses, in addition to the traditional use of polls, I used polls to provide information that would help improve the courses and to give the learners a voice.

After each module in a course, each learner was asked to rate a series of questions from one to five stars, including an option to explain their feedback. The questions could be anything from asking how they liked a new feature to asking if the content provided value to their work. Afterwards we could go into the back-end and see the ratings. If the ratings were bad, it was possible for us to see why the learner thought it was bad and what we should correct. And if the ratings were good, we could see what we should do more of.

This use of polls enabled BESTSELLER to continuously improve their courses and to develop them in a way that addressed the learner's preferences for learning. Furthermore, through the learner's contribution and by giving them a voice, each learner felt ownership and that they were part of something bigger. They weren't just participants, but co-creators helping to improve the course for future learners.

23. Lundbeck

I worked with Lundbeck on projects including transformation of their leadership programmes from webinar-based lectures (information dump) to experiential programmes that engaged managers, produced a higher learning outcome, and made a difference for their employees. I redesigned the programmes by adding case studies and infusing the pre-reading materials with theory, reflective questions, discussions, and planning assignments. The cases provided a context for understanding the theory. The reflective questions helped managers change their opinions about the theory. Sharing their reflections with their peer managers and the instructor and talking about how to apply the learning on the job created interactivity that was far more effective than the old-style information dump.

The programme culminated with the managers creating a six-month plan detailing how they would apply the new learning on the job. They met at the end of the six months to share experiences and results.

My work with Lundbeck led to several invitations to speak and present to other HR networks, external stakeholders, and some major companies in Denmark including LEGO and Maersk. This is what led me to launch my business—focussed, of course, on the design and development of online learning programmes for corporate and organisational settings.

What, Why, How for Lundbeck's Leadership Programme

The leadership programme was about setting direction and goals. I needed insight into the material to understand the scope, and I needed to help the Lundbeck team to reflect upon the programme and to think in new ways about what it should contain. To assist in this process I ran a *what, why,* and *how* exercise. The following example illustrates a single topic—setting direction and goals—within the whole course.

WHAT

What's the module about?

- *Helping managers understand why we set direction and goals.*

What do the managers have to know?

- *The overall strategy of the department.*
- *What results they need to deliver.*

What are the learning goals for the managers?

- *To understand the purpose of setting direction and goals and what role they play in the bigger picture (organisational strategy).*
- *To develop skills to effectively evaluate their employees.*
- *To effectively self-evaluate themselves as managers.*

- *To be able to support and help their team.*

W<small>HY</small>

Why is it important for the managers to set direction and goals?

- *To ensure alignment between the work of their employees' and the strategies of the organisation. With alignment, work is more effective and efficient. With alignment, employees see more recognition, reward, and job satisfaction.*

Why is goal-setting an important skill for managers?

- *To create a motivated and high-performing team.*
- *To foster a sense of ownership and empowerment for each employee.*

How

To get at the *how* concept for the course, I started by reviewing the answers we came up with in response to the question, "How can the managers apply these learning goals?"

We then brainstormed ideas for teaching tools. Although we ran through many learning goals, I'll give just two examples for you.

First, you'll see the *how* question we asked ourselves, then you'll see a tool that we determined the managers could use to learn *how*. And finally, you will see an example of how we used the tool.

Goal One: Help managers understand why they should set direction and goals, as well as to make a connection between their role and the bigger-picture corporate strategy.

Question: How can we help the manager set direction and goals that align with those of the organisation?

Tool: Create a workbook that includes leading questions about organisational strategies, directions, and goals, with empty fields where each manager can describe how their work/area contributes to those goals. Include a page with example answers to prompt the learner.

Goal Two: To develop the skills to effectively evaluate their employees.

Question: How can we help the manager to evaluate the performance of employees on an ongoing basis?

Tool: Include a performance rating scale in the workbook, explanations of what each rating scale means and benchmarks for employees to reach to obtain each score.

70/20/10

After doing the *what*, *why*, and *how* process, we agreed to structure the course considering the 70/20/10 approach in the following way:

- We provided reading materials with an actual case study. This helped the managers to more easily make the connection between the theory and their work. We also included reflection assignments related to the case study.
- We created a webinar during which the managers shared their reflections.
- We helped the managers make a plan to implement and integrate their new knowledge into their daily work.

Here's how this translated into the 70/20/10 buckets.

LUNDBECK 10 PER CENT

- Course overview

- Why it was important to participate
- What they would be able to achieve with the course
- Case study
- Theory
- Assignment with reflective questions related to the case and to their own work.

We uploaded the reflective assignments to a shared drive and gave access to all participants. This meant they could access one another's assignments, helping them to apply the theory, as well as motivating and inspiring them to do their best.

LUNDBECK 20 PER CENT

- Webinar presenting timelines and discussion of the learner's assignments

LUNDBECK 70 PER CENT

- The learner develops their own plan to apply the new theory on the job and then report back.

Fleshing out the content for the course, we introduced an SME and outlined her expertise (Ethos). We included pre-work to introduce the managers to the programme, what it was about, and why it was important (orientating the learner). We then presented managers with theory (10 per cent) and a case study including a problem that needed solving (present content material). The case study elicited some emotion from employees that made the leaders want to help (Pathos). It was also the kind of case study that we knew all the managers would be familiar with (stimulating recall of prior knowledge).

Problem-solving exercises formed the bulk of the work (70 per cent). Through a series of written questions, we asked the managers to use the theory to solve the problem. The questions were designed to help the learner reflect on their perceptions and beliefs as well as on the case study and its outcomes (provide learner guidance *and* elicit performance practice).

The managers shared their assignments to gain wider understanding and further inspiration (this helped to provide learner guidance *and* elicit performance practice *and* was part of the 20 per cent). This step also used the principle of social learning to support the managers. New knowledge was created, and community was strengthened.

Only then did the webinar take place. During the webinar, the participants presented key findings from their cases. The SME provided support and feedback (provide learner guidance).

After the webinar, we provided a guide to help the managers create a plan to apply the theory and new knowledge to their daily work (integration). Review work took place over the next six months with their leaders and determined how effectively the managers applied the knowledge in the workplace.

24. Henley Business School

Henley Business School in Denmark wanted to make its Master of Business Administration (MBA), ranked number three in the world, more accessible and engaging for the students. To help achieve this goal, Lars Hoffmann (who was then a learning designer and tutor at Henley) invited me to help transform part of Henley's executive MBA into an online course. Before I arrived, the MBA included a mix of readings, classroom lectures and assessment. Students would pre-read theory and case-studies from a workbook, then attend theory-based classroom lectures that included discussion of the workbook pre-readings and multiple-choice quizzes.

My work included converting theory from the workbook into videos, optimising the multiple-choice quizzes, and adding peer assessment. These changes aimed to help the learner *understand* and *apply* the theory, rather than just remember it. And, of course, I employed the 70/20/10 approach.

Original program:

- Self-study:
- Read text-based theory in a workbook (*part of the 10 per cent*)
- Read case-studies related to the theory in a workbook (*part of the 10 per cent*)
- Classroom
- Lecture (*part of the 10 per cent*)
- Discuss theory and case-studies (*part of the 20 per cent*)
- Multiple-choice quiz to check recall of theory

Revised program:

- Self-study:
- Watch videos explaining theory (*part of the 10 per cent*)
- Multiple-choice quiz to see if they could *understand* the theory, and receive feedback and explanation whether their answer was right or wrong
- Read case studies related to the theory (*part of the 10 per cent*)
- Apply the theory to case studies (*part of the 70 per cent*) and giving and receiving feedback from their peers (*part of the 20 per cent*)
- Classroom
- Discuss the case-studies with the teacher (*part of the 20 per cent*)

My Work (and Mistakes) With the Videos

When I submitted my proposal to Hoffmann and Henley Business School, I purposefully bid low. I really wanted the project. To fit my reduced budget, I chose to skip the *what, why,* and *how* process. Instead, I converted text from the workbooks, which already contained a *what,* into scripts we then filmed. In hindsight, this was a mistake. The videos were boring and generated low engagement rates. It taught me the importance and power of the *what, why, how* process and I've never skipped it again.

Multiple Choice Quizzes

The original classroom lectures only included multiple-choice quizzes that tested the participants' ability to remember and helped them to move knowledge from the short-term to the long-term memory about the facts.

With the perspective that knowledge is more valuable when you know how to apply it, we added multiple-choice quizzes that prompted the MBA students to reflect on how to apply the theory. Some of the new quizzes began with a question (example one below), while others presented a situation they'd have to understand before they'd be able to answer (example two below). We also added explanations so they would know why their answers were right or wrong. And we gave them a chance to revise an incorrect answer. If they answered correctly on the first try, they'd receive three points. If they answered incorrectly on the first try and correctly on the second try, they would receive one point. This motivated the MBA students to read carefully the feedback on their incorrect answers and review course materials before answering again.

ORIGINAL QUIZ QUESTION, SAMPLE ONE:
Question: What causes leaders to become overburdened and derail their success?

1. *Long-buried psychological damage showing up as erratic, unpredictable behaviour*

2. *Overexposure, over promotion, and excessive intellectual demands (correct)*
3. *Low emotional intelligence*

REVISED QUIZ QUESTION, SAMPLE ONE:
Question: How should leaders approach values conflict within the organisation?

1. *Upper-level management team aligns the values of the team with the vision, mission, and strategy and then shares that throughout the organisation (correct)*
2. *This is an inevitable consequence of a fundamental dilemma that cannot be addressed*
3. *Ensure their own personal brand values (PBV) are adopted across the organisation as a whole*

Explanatory feedback:

1. *Yes. While conflicts will always arise, they can be used constructively through dialogue and alignment.*
2. *No. While dilemmas exist, people and organisations can work better with the right approach to the conflicts they generate.*
3. *No. But you must recognise your Personal Brand Values before addressing value conflicts within the organisation.*

REVISED QUIZ QUESTION, SAMPLE TWO:
Situation: A team of executives spend their meetings in the following way: First, they all report on the work in their area or depart-ment. Second, the chief executive energetically presents key strategic

issues and directives. Third, a competitive discussion ends with the CEO making the final decisions regarding the accountability of each member of the group on the issue.

Question: A leadership team functioning in this way is:

1. *A transactional management group (correct)*
2. *A transformational leadership team*
3. *A transformational management team*

Peer Assessment What, How, and Why

One of the goals was to change the MBA students' opinions about some leadership tasks and about their habits. To achieve this, we needed them to apply their knowledge and think critically about its application. In the original program, students didn't have an opportunity to apply their knowledge as there was no "70" of the 70/20/10 approach. We used peer assessment to bring in the "70," helping them apply their knowledge by solving the problems posed in the case studies, to think critically about how they solved the case problems and why they should act in a certain (and in most cases new) way. This reflection process, in particular around the *why*, is what led them to change their opinions and habits.

Here's an example of a peer assessment exercise from the Henley MBA:

Situation: refer to the central case study involving a merger [which they would have read at this point of the programme].

Task: You should use the resources from Module One to identify what the main leadership problem was in this merger context. Feel free to use examples to illustrate your points.

1. *What were the main causes of the crisis from a change leadership perspective? (minimum 50 words)*
2. *How could Mr. Lithander have avoided the crisis from a change leadership perspective? (minimum 150 words)*

3. *Why do crises like the one in the merger occur?*
(minimum 100 words)

As you can see, we posed the *why* question after the *what* and *how* questions. If we asked the *why* question first, it would have no context and be too abstract to offer real value for the students. We also required a minimum number of words to encourage sufficient reflection.

After submitting their answers to the question, each MBA student would share their submission with two others and would in turn receive submissions to review from two of their peers. We created guidelines to help the students provide quality assessments to their peers.

Here's an excerpt from the Henley MBA peer assessment guidelines:

Assessment guidelines (you can choose one of the answers):

Distinction (5 points): Provides excellent analysis of the change process undertaken. Uses several theories from the module and key resources. Communicates with clarity and explicitly differentiates between theory, personal opinions or experience and case material.

Merit (3 points): Good analysis of the change process undertaken. Used several theories from the core module. Communicates and differentiates theory, personal opinions, or experience and case material well.

Pass (2 points): Adequate analysis of the change process taken. Limited use of theories and frameworks. Does not mix up theory, personal opinions or experience and case material.

Fail (0 points): Poor analysis of the change process undertaken. Little or no use of theories or frameworks. It's difficult to see where the submission refers to theory, personal opinions, experience, or case material.

25. Aarhus University

J eppe and I worked on a blended course in "Pursuing Entrepreneurship" for Aarhus University (which the Times Higher Education rated 127th on their list of the best universities in the world in 2019). The project was a success. Every student who participated recommended the course to fellow students. The course has also been translated into English and shared with another teaching institutions.

Purpose

The overall purpose of the course was to foster entrepreneurship skills through practice and hands-on experience. The learners were university and college students attracted to entrepreneurship. The course aimed to encourage more focus on taking action and less on the quality of the business idea.

Blended Course Structure

Access to resources at the university made it possible to plan in-person workshops before and after the course. This is known as the sandwich approach.

LAYER ONE

THE FIRST LAYER WAS A WORKSHOP WHERE WE INTRODUCED THE students to entrepreneurship, created a safe environment, and encouraged them to take action.

PHYSICAL WORKSHOP (DAY ONE):

- Professors introduced "Pursuing Entrepreneurship"
- Keynote speaker
- We divided the students into groups of eight
- We provided a manual with tools for practicing entrepreneurship

LAYER TWO (CONTENT)

THE SECOND LAYER, WHICH WE CALLED THE WORK ZONE, comprised the bulk of the course. We delivered SMS text messages with links to videos containing theory, tools, and exercises. These messages contained a brief description of the content followed by a link to a YouTube playlist.

. . .

WORK ZONE (DAYS TWO TO THIRTEEN)

- Course material
- Exercises

LAYER THREE

FOURTEEN DAYS AFTER THE FIRST WORKSHOP, WE HELD A second workshop. The purpose of this second workshop was to enable reflection, which is key to learning from experience. It's also the process where input moves from short- to long-term memory. Here, we focussed the students' attention on what they had learned, helping them merge the new learning with their existing knowledge.

PHYSICAL WORKSHOP (DAY FOURTEEN):

- Evaluation and reflection
- Keynote speaker
- Next steps

So that's what the delivery of the course looked like. Here's how we planned the elements.

Learning Goals

Our first step in planning the course content was to work with the professors to establish the overall learning goals of the course. Even though the professors already had an idea of the learning goals, we facilitated a brainstorming exercise that fostered new perspectives and ideas about the learning goals. We started the process by writing all ideas for learning goals on a whiteboard. We then removed the least important and combined the remaining into three overall learning goals:

- Learning goal one: commit to an idea
- Learning goal two: pitching the idea
- Learning goal three: understanding customer needs

With the learning goals in hand, our next step was to conduct a *what, why, how* process.

What, Why, How Process

Learning Goal One: Commit to an Idea
What?

- *Entrepreneurship is about solving problems*
- *Ideas will always change and develop*
- *It's impossible to say if an idea is good or bad*
- *Identifying ideas means having an open mind*

Why?

- *Each learner needs an idea to work with in the course*

How?

- *We'd use the needs, approach, benefit, and competition (NABC) model to articulate the ideas.*

THE NABC MODEL HELPS THE LEARNER REFLECT ABOUT

problem solving and explain their idea in a way their audience understands.

Need: what are the customer and market needs?

Approach: what's your unique approach for addressing this need?

Benefit: what are the specific benefits for the stakeholder?

Competition: how are the benefits superior to the competition or alternatives?

LEARNING GOAL TWO: PITCHING THE IDEA
What?

- *Pitching the idea*
- *Developing the idea*
- *Getting the resources (knowledge or materials) one needs to start*
- *Practicing talking about the idea*

Why?

- *Receiving feedback to develop one's idea*
- *Getting help from unexpected sources*

How?

- *Using a developed NABC-model for pitching*

The NABC model would include:

- *A hook: an introduction that 'hooks' the listener's attention.*
- *Needs: the need addressed by the product or service.*
- *Approach: how they will solve the need.*
- *Benefit: the benefit(s) of using the product or service.*

- *Competition: how the new product or service differs from competitors.*
- *Closure: a strong finish line the listener will remember.*

LEARNING GOAL THREE: UNDERSTANDING CUSTOMER NEEDS
What?

- *Testing hypotheses (in common language assumptions)*
- *Identifying the customers' jobs, pains, and gains*

Why?

- *To ensure the idea solves a problem and creates value for the customer*
- *To test if customers will pay for the idea*
- *To test if customers prefer feature A, B, or C*

How?

- *Using a value proposition (VP) canvas (a tool to understand the customer's needs and design products and services they want).*
- *Using a hypotheses card (a tool to structure one's hypotheses in order to test them with customers).*
- *Using a learning card (a tool to capture learnings from the hypotheses tests and make the resulting decisions and actions explicit).*

Pedagogical Tools

With the learning goals and the *what, why, how* process complete, we were ready to identify which pedagogical tools to use to create a meaningful learning experience for the students.

70/20/10

As I do with all the courses I create, we planned a variation on the 70/20/10 approach for Pursuing Entrepreneurship.

The 20 per cent: theory through video.

The 60 per cent: applying the theory in practice.

The 20 per cent: discussing and reflecting upon the use of the theory.

PROBLEM-BASED LEARNING

We incorporated content that included situations (problems) the students would encounter in real life, such as pitching their idea to people they know and don't know, to those who can provide feedback to help shape and develop their idea, and to investors for raising money.

STORYTELLING

We engaged storytelling and identified real-life examples from well-known entrepreneurs that would help the students understand the problems and motivate them to find solutions. Instructors would explain how these entrepreneurs have benefited from using the methods the students were about to learn in Pursuing Entrepreneurship. We planned work for the students following a progression of inter-related tasks, working from the least to the most complex problems.

APPLICATION

Applying new knowledge or skill to real-world tasks is a necessary condition for effective learning. To create a connection between the theory taught in Pursuing Entrepreneurship and real-life practice, the students needed to solve explicit tasks. We arranged for students to film themselves doing the tasks. They'd then upload their video to the Facebook group as a required part of the learning activities.

DEMONSTRATION

In Pursuing Entrepreneurship, we incorporated two types of demonstration: behavioural (how to do things) and cognitive (why use the knowledge/skill).

We included videos so students could see how to use the knowledge and theory in practice, such as animations showing how to write an NABC model and real-life examples from two entrepreneurs performing a pitch. Using videos for the behavioural demonstrations made sense because a pitch is a live performance, and the students would be able to re-watch the demonstrations as many times as they wanted when practicing and filming their own pitch.

The Pursuing Entrepreneurship cognitive demonstration would include video interviews with two young Danish entrepreneurs (my friends Allan and Nichlas who own the company Swap Language) just out of university and to whom the students could relate, sharing their own experience with entrepreneurship. Using video for the cognitive demonstrations helped to evoke pathos, making it more likely the students would listen to and learn from the two young entrepreneurs' experiences.

REFLECTION

To facilitate a reflective process for the students in Pursuing Entrepreneurship, we also arranged for the students to film their own pitch and give feedback to one another rather than receiving instructor feedback.

With the pedagogical tools and the *what, why, how* process complete, we could start writing the scripts.

Script Outline

Here is the outline we developed for the scripts.
Introduction

- *Introduction of the professors*

Learning Goal One: Commit to an Idea

- *Put vanity aside*
- *Commit to your idea*
- *Make your idea more specific*
- *Example of NABC – Swap Language*
- *The beginning of an entrepreneurship journey – Interview with Swap Language*
- *Exercise: Create an NABC model*

Learning Goal Two: Pitching the Idea

- *Develop your idea further*
- *Acquire resources*
- *Prepare your pitch*
- *Pitch example – Swap Language*
- *Why talk about your idea? Interview with Swap Language*
- *Exercise: film yourself performing a pitch*

Learning Goal Three: Understanding Customer Needs

- *Understand your customer's needs*
- *Introduction to VP canvas*

- *Hypothesis test example*
- *Learning card example*
- *Why test your hypothesis? Interview with Swap Language*
- *Exercises: create a VP canvas, learning card, and hypothesis card with your own idea*

EXTRACTS FROM THE SCRIPTS

Why every idea has merit and why you should put vanity aside:

Example: In 1991 BIC pens added a small hole in the cap. Many people were biting the cap off the pen. While the risk was low, if the cap was swallowed it was possible for it to cut off the airway. The hole in the cap made it possible to breathe, even if the cap made it into a person's airways. The little idea that sounded stupid at first has helped save lives.
The point is that no matter how bad an idea may sound, it may turn out to be really good. Perhaps it can even save human life. It does not really make sense to talk about whether an idea is good or bad from the start. Therefore, I would urge you to identify ideas with an open mind and not shoot down an idea before giving it a try. You will only find out if your idea is good or bad by working with it.

How an idea can develop:

Example one: Netflix started as a DVD movie rental company. It is said that co-founder Reed Hastings was tired of getting fines when he handed his films in late to Blockbuster. It was too complicated to enter the store and deliver them. Netflix made it easier for the customer to receive and return their movies by mail.
Today, Netflix is one of the world's largest online streaming

services of movies and comics. They changed the problem they were going to solve and the idea they had to solve the problem. Most importantly, they committed themselves to their idea. If they had not done that, Netflix would not exist today.

Example two: It's when you come out and talk to others about your idea that its development really takes place. It brings your idea into focus and helps it evolve. When you talk to others about your idea, their feedback may open up new opportunities you would not otherwise see.
Let's look at the company Rains as an example of an evolving idea. The founders of Rains saw a problem: rainwear is ugly and never fashionable. I certainly never thought that the lack of fashionable rainwear was a problem. Rainwear is rainwear. I would never have thought by solving the problem I didn't know existed you could create a million-dollar business in just a few years.
Today, Rains is an established brand with millions in sales. Rains may not be a little start-up anymore, but their idea has evolved. Today you can buy fashionable rainwear, as well as fashionable waterproof bags and accessories.
We must remind ourselves that the bold companies and products we see today started somewhere else and as something else. They changed course again and again before becoming what they are today.
The idea has evolved, and the same will happen to your idea when you talk about it.
We must be very careful about judging each other's ideas because an idea is constantly evolving.

Why you want to tell other people about your idea in order to get resources (knowledge or materials):

Example: It may be that you already know what type of

resources you need, but often, at first, your idea is unformed and unclear, and you don't know what you need. It's when talking to others about your idea and through their feedback that you become wiser about what resources you need. And it's through talking about your idea that you gain access to valuable resources.

Excerpt from interview with Swap Language (cognitive demonstration) about why you should tell other people about your idea:

Sometimes you get help from unexpected places. Some time ago Allan and I hitchhiked around Europe to spread our message and vision. During our trip in Spain we went from Barcelona to Valencia, and we had no place to stay in Valencia. Fortunately, Allan came to think of a guy we had met in Copenhagen the previous year, and we thought he lived in Valencia. When we met him in Copenhagen, we talked for ten minutes about Swap Language and then we exchanged business cards. And we hadn't spoken since. The next time he heard from us was two hours before we arrived in Valencia. That same evening, we sat on his terrace overlooking the ocean, drinking red wine and discussing business models all night long. He turned out to be an IT millionaire who enjoys life in Spain. That opportunity only arose because we had talked about our idea!

26. Bimco

I was asked to do a review and critique of existing online training material for Bimco, the Baltic and International Maritime Council. Bimco, an NGO, is the world's largest international shipping organisation with more than 2,000 members in over 120 countries.

Members may be ship owners, operators, managers, brokers, or agents.

The feedback I provided to Bimco may be helpful to you as you embark on developing your own online learning course. What follows is the near-verbatim material I provided to them.

Challenges

I began my report to Bimco outlining the challenges I saw with the courses.

Too Much Information

When there is too much information that's not linked to a context, theory remains/becomes abstract.

Not Emphasising a *Why*

Not understanding what I will be able to *do* after the course, only what I will *know* can lead to lower engagement and motivation.

Not Emphasising a *How*

If the learner can't see how the theory can be used to solve challenges, they'll have difficulty using the course to solve their own and improve their work.

No "Bigger Picture"

This makes it difficult to navigate and contextualise the information in the course.

Not Explaining the Rules

When you don't explain the rules of the course, for example what's expected from the learner and their involvement, and the purpose, you risk creating a chaotic learning experience.

Teaching for the Test

Final quizzes are not helping the learner achieve a higher learning outcome. Contemporary research in assessment indicates that continuous assessment leads to significantly better learning results. And that continuous assessment combined with end assessment leads to even better learning results.

Only Summative Assessment

Incorporating only summative assessment doesn't provide guidance to the learner.

No Opportunity to Reflect on Theory

This inhibits the transfer of experience from the short- to the long-term memory, doesn't activate the whole brain, and reduces the learning outcomes because it doesn't change the learner's workplace behaviour.

Lack of Structure

Lack of structure makes it time consuming to understand the purpose and makes assessments confusing to solve.

No Subtitles

Subtitles are a big help for people whose native language is not English. Hearing *and* seeing helps some learners understand the content better.

Suggestions for Improvement

My recommendations for Bimco to improve their course offerings, learner experience, and results are as follows:

Incorporate Case-Based Learning

Why: case-based learning is used to connect theory to practice. Connecting theory to a practical situation will result in a learning experience where:

- theory is less abstract, more tangible.
- learners can create a connection between theory and practice.
- learners can see a connection through the material in the entire module.

How? Tell a story about a company, or a ship that's sailing around the world, and that while underway faces the challenges listed in the some of your internal documents.
Include:

- Why it met this challenge.
- What the challenge is.
- How to solve the challenge.

Use Storytelling

Why: storytelling can be used as part of a case-based learning exercise to catch the learner's attention and to help the learner understand *why*. As part of your storytelling, talk to:

- Logos: appeals to logic and offers credible evidence to support arguments
- Pathos: emotional influence and appeals to the learner's emotions

Choose the subject of your story based on something that has happened in real life, rather than an imaginary scenario. This makes it more authentic and emphasises the connection to pathos.

How? Explain how the situation occurred, and how law/theory was used to solve it.

· · ·

Graphic Visualisations

Why: using icons, images, or still photos as additional layers in the video can:

- Make videos more engaging
- Invoke pathos
- Some research claims that the average attention span is eight seconds. We get bored and move after only eight seconds of reading, listening, or seeing and our brains will switch off if not constantly entertained. Adding visuals can help keep the brain entertained, attentive, and interested.

How? Use pictures or visuals where and when it makes sense. Consider both images and text that sums up key facts or numbers.

Continuous Assessment

Why: the learner should know if they have understood the theory – or not – immediately after watching/reading a video/text. They should also have a chance to recap immediately to get on the right track.

How? Insert a quiz after each video or segment of text.

Formative Quizzes

Why: to help the learner identify their strengths and weaknesses and whether they've understood the material. Formative quizzes should be guiding and help the learner immediately address their knowledge gap.

How? Include quizzes that provide the learner with an explanation of the correct answer, addressing why their answer is either right or wrong.

. . .

Behaviour Quizzes

Why: to assess behaviour and not only memory.

How? Illustrate a narrative and ask how the learner would act in a given situation.

Example one: assessment for students studying to become a physiotherapist.

A fit-looking thirty-five-year-old office worker smokes cigarettes. He comes to you to complain of cramps in his left leg when playing tennis. Which of the following are likely causes of his cramps?

1. *Muscle spasm*
2. *Tendon rupture*
3. *Psychogenic pain*

Which question would lead you to a diagnosis of his problem?

1. *How long has the problem persisted?*
2. *Do you suffer from diabetes?*
3. *Does it only come when you are playing tennis?*

Example two: assessment in retail.

This new Christmas knit features a cotton/cashmere blend. Why would you tell the consumer that this is an upgraded quality?

1. *Because it ensures a strong and warm quality*
2. *Because it adds a soft touch while still being lightweight*
3. *Because it adds a soft and warm quality* (correct)

If wrong:

*No. That is not correct. When adding cashmere into cotton,
the fabric becomes softer and warmer. A cool fact you can
share with the consumer is that the cashmere goat only gives
180 grams of hair per year.*

PROBLEM-BASED ASSESSMENT

Why: in addition to quizzes, problem-based assessment can be
used to stimulate additional parts of the brain, leading to a higher
learning outcome and behaviour change.

How? Present the learner with a case they have to solve:

- Present a story that has a connection to the module
- Ask a question that relates to *what, why,* and *how*

EXAMPLE: LEADERSHIP AND CHANGE COURSE.

*Task: Using the resources from the merger crisis example provided
in the module, identify what the main leadership problem was in the
context of this merger. Feel free to use examples to illustrate your
points.*

1. *What were the main causes of the crisis from a change
   leadership perspective? (Minimum 50 words.)*
2. *How could this crisis have been avoided, from a change
   leadership perspective? (Minimum 150 words.)*
3. *Why do crises like the one in the merger occur?
   (Minimum 100 words.)*

27. Review the Five Steps

T
o help tie all the information in *Achieving Change* together
and reinforce what you've read, here is a summary review
of the five steps to supercharge your online learning. Along
your journey, check in with this summary chapter for reminders of
what's next and what to prepare for. You'll know which chapter to go
back to if you need to refresh your memory in more detail.

First, a recap about what scientific research in this area tells us:

- Pedagogy is more important than technology
- Interaction between participants has a positive effect on
  the learning outcome
- Online courses work well for adult education
- "Group project work and peer grading: engaging, critical
  to learning"[1]

Step One: Know the Learning Brain

THE FOUR BRAIN QUADRANTS

As learning designers, we want to know *how* the brain learns so that we can create learning experiences that enables the learner to move information from short- to long-term memory and ultimately *act* in new ways on the job.

Learning activates four parts of the brain:

1. Frontal cortex – abstract hypotheses
2. Aft frontal lobe – motor skills
3. Occipital and parietal lobes – concrete experiences
4. Temporal lobe – reflective observation

The four approaches that correspond to each part of the brain:

1. Present content for practical application (frontal integrative cortex).
2. Provide ways for the learner to apply theory or tools into practice (occipital and parietal lobes, aft section of frontal lobe).
3. Include scenarios for the learner to reflect on the practical application and assess how it went (temporal lobe).
4. Include scenarios for the learner to reflect on how they can improve their results (temporal lobe).

THREE TYPES OF LEARNING

1. Assimilative: when a learner receives the information, the brain immediately finds which box to put the information into. See dog, say dog.
2. Accommodative: an active learning process where the brain adapts new knowledge to existing knowledge, resulting in a reconstruction of existing knowledge.
3. Transformative: occurs when people have experiences that change the way they understand the world and the result is the change of opinions, attitudes, and habits.

Social Learning

Learning happens through the exchange of ideas, information, and feedback between people. To co-create new knowledge, you must have a workplace, training content, and peers with whom you discuss the content in order to create knowledge and new meaning.

Experiential Learning

Learning by doing is the hands on, dig-right-in style of learning that quickly helps the learner translate the theoretical into the practical. When a learner can practice what they've just learned, it helps them remember the new ideas and concepts.

Experiential learning includes regular and critical reflection.

Regular reflection: each learner looks over new knowledge/experiences, considers how to use that information, and then applies it.

Critical reflection: each learner considers their opinions, attitudes, and habits, why they should change them, and then they change their behaviour based on new information.

70/20/10

The 70/20/10 model allows learners with different learning preferences to benefit equally, because it activates the learning brain in four different ways:

1. getting information
2. activating the information
3. reflecting on what's occurred, or on the new information
4. abstractly or critically reflecting on how to improve next time

The guideline to follow is:

- Experience and on-the-job training: 70 per cent
- Group work activities: 20 per cent
- Courseware instruction and videos: 10 per cent

KNOWLEDGE, SKILLS, COMPETENCIES

Knowledge = ability to understand and remember
Skills = ability to apply and analyse
Competencies = ability to evaluate and create

Step Two: Initiate Course Development

Your goal is to enable learners to analyse, evaluate, apply, and create.

Your role is to extract the theoretical knowledge or tools from the SME's head and transfer it into a learning experience that helps people gain knowledge and use tools that achieve results.

Create a course overview that addresses:

- what the learning goals are for participants
- how you'll know if these goals are accomplished
- what the instructor and learner must do so that the learner achieves the learning goals
- the context of the learning situation, nature of the subject, and characteristics of both teacher and learner

WHAT, WHY, AND HOW

WHAT are the learning goals? What is it your employees must learn?

WHY are the learning goals important? Help the learner understand *why* the knowledge is important and *why* it will benefit them.

How will you help the learner achieve the learning goals? What tools will you use? Handouts, practical exercises, a video that illustrates how to carry out the *what*, or a simple brochure?

Step Three: Engage the Learner

Continually step into the learner's shoes and create a connection between the content and learner. Use "you," "us," and "we" language. Keep the *learner* at the centre of the course, not the content. Present material in a way that speaks to the learner: communicate so the learner can understand and apply.

Follow the four principles for creating engaging content:

1. PROBLEM-BASED: learning is promoted when a learner acquires skill in the context of real-world problems
2. DEMONSTRATION: learning is promoted when a learner observes a demonstration of the skill to be learned
3. APPLICATION: learning is promoted when a learner applies their newly-acquired skill to solve problems
4. INTEGRATION: learning is promoted when a learner reflects on and discusses their newly acquired skill

Incorporate the three modes of persuasion:
Ethos = trustworthy, reliable, competent and credible.
Pathos = storytelling, evocative of an emotional response.
Logos = logical and rational.

Step Four: Create the Scripts

Your scripts are the building blocks of your video content. In almost all cases, online learning involves presentation of course content via video.

- Start with why, and put yourself in the shoes of the learner

- Create a meaningful introduction
- Set the goal
- Establish credibility
- Explain what they'll learn
- Explain how they'll learn
- Explain how they'll be assessed

Structuring your Scripts

- Communicate the WHY
- Communicate the WHAT
- Communicate the HOW

Video

- Your online learning course should incorporate video whenever possible
- Rehearse your scripts and use a teleprompter
- Speak directly to the individual learner, not the masses
- Use authentic settings
- Pay attention to sound quality
- Remember "say dog, see dog." The words and video must match.

Step Five: Assessment for Learning

Measure learning, not participation, and not memory.
The four tools for assessment:

- Multiple choice: Questions and possible answers crafted from a basis of science, prompting the learner to consider how to apply the new knowledge.

- Polls help the learner engage in the course and to think critically about the content in the course, as they are able to see their own contribution as well as compare with others in the course.
- Peer instruction is a new generation of multiple choice with a social dimension.
- Peer assessment is the most useful assessment method in online learning to date, both for measuring and learning purposes. Peer assessment is participant-to-participant.

Assessment tools require an assessment mindset.

DEVELOP A LEARNER-CENTRED ASSESSMENT MINDSET

To achieve specific learning outcomes, facilitate different types of reflection.

Reflection can happen on three levels:

1. Reflection over content (what)
2. Reflection over the process (how)
3. Reflection over the premise for one's opinions, attitudes, and habits (why)

Peer assessment's dialogue and discussion enable critical reflection and the transformative learning that follows.

Summative assessment looks backward and asks if learners can remember. In formative assessment, learners explain their answers in writing and receive peer and instructor feedback that improves their learning.

Ongoing assessments provide opportunities for learners to continuously reflect, which helps them move the new knowledge from short- to long-term memory.

Situational assessments link content to a practical situation, assessing the learner's ability to apply the content.

Giving an explanation to the learner immediately after answering a question in a quiz helps the learner understand why an answer is wrong, what the correct answer is, and how to correct the misunderstanding.

Second attempt encourages learners to correct misunderstandings by earning fewer points on a second correct attempt than a first try.

WRITING MULTIPLE-CHOICE QUIZZES

Writing good multiple-choice is a science. Link to learning goals, qualify your questions, employ an appropriate level of complexity, write the central idea and avoid negative language.

Achieving Future Change

Once you adopt the five steps to supercharge online learning in your knowledge-driven organisation, you will be well equipped to help your employees grow, engage, and interact with peers. And they'll be more likely to want to stay with your organisation as you grow. You'll help your workers achieve greater workplace efficiency which, in turn, will produce meaningful and measurable return on investment for the company.

Remember that it isn't enough for your employees to know. If they are going to help you achieve change, they must also be able to act, to put into practice the new knowledge and skills.

What we need, especially in knowledge-driven organisations, are learning programmes that help improve the soft skills that are so critical in business. Talent attraction and retention along with corporate competition and innovation all rely on soft skills in leadership, management, and sales roles. Online learning, in an applied way, is an excellent format for soft-skills training.

Organisations and companies compete and achieve their goals when we consistently and effectively share knowledge. Students and employees learn through the exchange of information and ideas.

People create knowledge when they interact and have shared experiences. For example, attending a meeting is a form of social learning. You and your colleagues come to the meeting with different perspectives. In the end you will all have new knowledge fostered through social activity.

Digital learning can be available anywhere, anytime, for anyone who wants it. When you're investing in its design, creation, and delivery, and you want a solid return on that investment, it makes sense to combine pedagogy with technology to ensure you're achieving change.

What about evolving technology? Technological advancements such as virtual reality (VR), augmented reality (AR), and artificial intelligence (AI) stand to further transform the learning landscape. Company leaders will invest billions of dollars developing new ways to deliver teaching and learning programs using the new technologies.

If these leaders, and others financing the development of learning via VR, AR, and AI fail to remember to consider how the end user learns, they will fail. At least at first.

No matter what technological advancement we will see in the future, the *Achieving Change* approach will remain relevant. The five steps presented in *Achieving Change* are not bound to any specific technology, rather they are bound to how the brain works and how humans learn by nature. Technology might change rapidly, but the human brain won't. As a learning designer you still need to address the four different parts of the brain when you teach, no matter if it's through in-classroom instruction or VR.

However, new technologies do offer the potential for facilitating greater learning experiences. For instance, VR could enable us to turn case studies into real world experiences, and AI could facilitate instant reflection and conversations without the need for peers or instructors.

As a learning designer and a person interested in technology, I look forward to embracing the future of online learning and to leveraging technology to create learning experiences more engaging for learners of the future. And I hope that you will use the *Achieving Change* approach and achieve great results, no matter what technology you use.

To help you on your journey of creating engaging online learning, I encourage you join the LinkedIn Group: *Achieving Change with Online Learning*. Here, you can get inspiration as well as feedback on your own challenges from several learning enthusiasts, including me, and the people who have endorsed this book. I hope to see you in the group!

If You've Enjoyed This Book

If you've enjoyed reading this book, please take a moment and return to the seller's platform where you bought the book, and leave an honest review? That helps other readers decide whether the book is right for them. Thank you.

Henrik

Acknowledgments

I would not be where I am today, and this book wouldn't have been possible, without my former business partner and co-founder Jeppe Guldager. I've learned a lot from you and from our endless discussion about learning theory. A lot of things have happened in our lives since we gave our first presentations about MOOCs, since we created our first online education for the Fairstart Foundation, and since we started a company together. Jeppe, it has been a fun, sometimes hard, but very educational journey. I want to thank you for your patience, your kindness, and for being the inspiring character you are.

I want to thank Tommy V. Christiansen and his wife Bodil for putting their trust in Jeppe and I and for including us in the process of building a company. Tommy, the most important thing I've learned from you is your approach to creating a company: ethics first, quality second, and money third. Thank you for teaching me these values and showing me how to practice them in my every day life.

Thank you Boni and John from Ingenium Books for being a part of this book adventure, and for our endless talks, discussions, and revisions. Without your patience, understanding, and especially engagement, this book wouldn't have the quality it ended up having.

Thank you to Frank Høedt for providing the illustrations for Achieving Change. Frank is one of Denmark's best, most highly-skilled illustrators supporting online learning videos with drawings and animations.

I also owe a big thank you to my current co-founder, Anika Leth. Thank you for your patience when I've had to attend meetings with Ingenium Books, and for your understanding when I've been tired on a Monday morning after a long weekend of writing.

To my family. Thank you, Dad, for always welcoming me with fresh-baked buns and homemade jam. I really enjoy the time we spend together and to relax in your company.

Thank you, nieces and nephews, for always being up for playing with your uncle, and to my siblings for your understanding of my entrepreneurial life. The time I've spent with my family during the process of writing this book has been a place where I could relax and collect the energy needed to write this book after long days of work.

And finally, my closest friends. You know who you are. When being passionate about your company and sometimes working seventy to 100 hours per week, it can be difficult to find time to maintain friendships. However, I've found out that it is important to have good friends to keep your head up in the busy times. I want to thank you for always being there, for never talking about work when we are together, and instead talking about things that make us laugh. You've taught me the importance of friendship and you've taught me that people are not what they do for a living, but how they respond to others. Thank you for your understanding and support. I wouldn't have accomplished much or be where I am today without you.

About the Author

Other than biking, having "hygge," and picking apples with his dad in his garden, there's nothing Henrik J. Mondrup likes better than working on his life's goal: improving people's lives through online education and *achieving change*.

Whether he's working with a third-world non-profit organisation that's trying to improve the quality of life for the orphaned children in its care, or a multi-national corporation that's trying to change workplace practices and improve overall productivity, Mondrup facilitates *achieving change* through design of online courses that incorporate socialisation with the latest learning theories and technology tools. The impact is powerful and the resulting change is lasting and meaningful.

Mondrup is a sought-after international speaker, having presented at conferences and events across North America and Europe and hosted by organisations such as Harvard University and MIT, Rotary International, the British Chamber of Commerce in Denmark, universities and more. He has a BS in Education Science and a MS in IT and Learning from Aalborg University in Copenhagen, Denmark.

Connect with Henrik on LinkedIn: https://www.linkedin.com/in/henrikjmondrup/

Bibliography

Al-Atabi, M. and J. DeBoer. "Teaching entrepreneurship using Massive Open Online Course (MOOC)." 2014.

Admiraal, W., B. Huisman, and O. Pilli. "Assessment in Massive Open Online Courses." 2015.

Alonso-Betanzos, A., A. Bahamonde, J. Díes, O. Luaces, and A. Troncoso. A "Factorization Approach to Evaluate Open-response Assignments in MOOCs Using Preference Learning on Peer Assessments." 2015.

Aristotle, W. Rhys Roberts, Ingram Bywater, Friedrich Solmsen, and Aristotle. 1954. Rhetoric. New York: Modern Library.

Bazil, V. and A. Petras. Worte und Werte. In V. Bazil and R. Wöller (Eds.), *Rede als Führungsinstrument*. Gabler. 2008.

Bloom, B. S. Taxonomy of Educational Objectives: The Classification of Educational Goals. Handbook 1; Cognitive Domain. New York: David McKay Co. Inc., 1956.

Bruun, J., Reinecker, L. (2013). Feedback. In Dolin, J., Ingerslev, G. H., Joergensen J. S., Reinecker, L. (Eds.), Universitetspaedagogik. Gylling: Narayana Press.

Canelas, D.A., C.R. Clark, and D.K. Comer. "Writing to Learn and Learning to Write Across the Disciplines: Peer-to-Peer Writing in Introductory-level MOOCs." 2014.

Chen, D., Y. Feng, J. Jiang, J. Yu, and Z. Zhao. "Does MOOC Really Work Effectively." 2014.

Christensen, C., M. B. Horn, and C. W. Johnson. *Disrupting Class: How Disruptive Innovation Will Change the Way the World Learns.* New York: McGraw-Hill, 2008.

Commission, E. "The European Qualifications Framework for Life-long Learning." Retrieved from European Commission: http://eose.org/wp-content/uploads/2014/02/Leaflet-EQF.pdf. 2008, October.

Cranton, P. *Understanding and promoting transformative learning* (Second Edition). San Francisco: Jossey-Bass, 2006.

Dalsgaard, C. *Åbne læringsressourcer - mod en sociokulturel teori om læringsressourcer.* Ph.D. thesis. 2007.

Digital Marketing Institute. The value and importance of online learning. https://digitalmarketinginstitute.com/en-us/the-insider/the-value-and-importance-of-online-learning.

Eimler, S. C., N.C. Krämer, G. Neubaum, and A. Wichmann. "Investigating Incentives for Students to Provide Peer Feedback in a Semi-Open Online Course: An Experimental Study." 2014.

Fink, L. D. Integrated Course Design. "Idea Paper #42." The IDEA Center. 2005.

Gagne, R. *The Conditions of Learning*. New York: Holt, Rinehart & Winston. 1985.

Ganapathy, S. "MindTickle." Retrieved from https://www.mindtickle.com/blog/new-research-moocs-impacts-training-millennials/. 2017.

Frett, D. "Gen Y Women in the Workplace - Focus Group Summary Report." Business and Professional Women's (BPW) Foundation. 2011.

Giles, H., and P. F. Powesland. *Speech Style and Social Evaluation*. London and New York: Academic Press. 1975.

Glance, D. G., Forsey, M., & Riley, M. (2013). The pedagogical foundations of massive open online courses. *First Monday, 18*(5), 1-12.

Grady, C. L., A. R. McIntosh, M. N. Rajah, and F. I. Craik. "Neural correlates of the episodic encoding of pictures and words." Proceedings of the National Academy of Sciences of the United States of America, 95(5), 2703-2708. doi:10.1073/pnas.95.5.2703. 1998.

Haladyna, T. M., & Rodriguez, M. C. (2013). *Developing and Validating Test Items*. Routledge.

Handley, L. CNBC. Retrieved from https://www.cnbc.-

com/2017/06/01/sebastian-thrun-udacity-googlex.html.   2017,
June 1.

Holcomb, P. J., and J. Grainger. "On the time course of visual word
recognition: an event-related potential investigation using masked
repetition priming." Journal of Cognitive Neuroscience, 1631-1643.
doi:10.1162/jocn.2006.18.10.1631. 2006, October.

Illeris, K. *How We Learn: Learning and Non-Learning in School and
Beyond.* Abingdon: Routledge. 2007.

Jasmini V. "Online learning statistics and trends." Retrieved from
eLearning Industry: https://elearningindustry.com/online-learning-
statistics-and-trends. 2017, August 13.

Kolb, D. A. *Experiential Learning: Experience as the Source of
Learning and Development.* Upper Saddle River, New Jersey: FT
Press. 1984.

Lombardo, Michael M., and Robert W. Eichinger. *The Career Archi-
tect Development Planner: A Systematic Approach to Development
including 103 Research-based and Experience-tested Development
Plans and Coaching Tips for Learners, Managers, Mentors, and Feedback Givers.* Minneapolis, MN: Lominger International, a
Korn/Ferry Company, 2010.

Luo, H., J. Park, and A.C. Robinson. "Peer Grading in a MOOC:
Reliability, Validity and Perceived Effects." 2014.

*Millennial Careers: 2020 Vision Facts, Figures and Practical Advice
from Workforce Experts.* Report. Manpower Group. 2016. Accessed
April 30, 2019. https://www.manpowergroup.com/wps/wcm/con-
nect/660ebf65-144c-489e-975c-9f838294c237/MillennialsPa-
per1_2020Vision_lo.pdf?MOD=AJPERES.

Margaryan, A., M. Bianco, and A. Littlejohn. Instructional quality of Massive Open Online Courses (MOOCs). "Computers & Education," pp. 77-83. 2015, January.

Merrill, M. First principles of instruction: Identifying and designing effective, efficient and engaging instruction. Hoboken, NJ: Pfeiffer/John Wiley & Sons. 2013.

Merrill,   M.D.   ETR&D   (2002)   50:   43. https://doi.org/10.1007/BF02505024

Mezirow, J. *Fostering Critical Reflection in Adulthood: A Guide to Transformative and Emancipatory learning.* (J. Mezirow, & Associates, Eds.) San Francisco: Jossey-Bass. 1990.

Mintzberg, Henry. *Simply Managing: What Managers Do - and Can Do Better.* Harlow, England: Pearson, 2013.

Mondrup, H. "Developing a design for transformative learning in a Global MOOC." Retrieved from http://projekter.aau.dk/projekter/files/222537577/Henrik.Jensen.Mondrup._20131779.Speciale.Artikel.docx. 2015, November.

Mondrup, H. J. "The Evolution of Multiple-Choice E-learning." Retrieved October 12, 2017, from LinkedIn: https://www.linkedin.com/pulse/evolution-multiple-choice-e-learning-henrik-j-mondrup/?trk=prof-post. 2016, September.

Nielson, B. "New MOOC Research: What the Findings Mean for Corporate Training." Retrieved from Your Training Edge: http://www.yourtrainingedge.com/new-mooc-research-what-the-findings-mean-for-corporate-training/. 2015, July.

Obama, B. "Remarks by the President at the National League of

Cities Conference." Retrieved from Obama White House Archives: https://obamawhitehouse.archives.gov/the-press-office/2015/03/09/remarks-president-national-league-cities-conference. 2015, March.

OECD. "Income inequality (indicator)." Retrieved from OECD.org: https://data.oecd.org/inequality/income-inequality.htm. 2017.

Pappas, C. "The Top eLearning Statistics and Facts For 2015 You Need to Know." Retrieved September 12, 2017, from eLearning Industry: https://elearningindustry.com/elearning-statistics-and-facts-for-2015. 2015, January 25.

Parsons, A. McKinsey Academy. Retrieved from https://www.slideshare.net/andysparsons/open-edx-conference-2014.

Peopleway. *Learning Impact Map.* Internal report created for Lundbeck.

Piaget, J. *The Essential Piaget.* New York: Basic Books (AZ). 1977.

Piaget, Jean. *Language and Thought of the Child.* Routledge, 2015.

Potter, M. C., B. Wyble, C. E. Hagmann, and E. S. McCourt. "Detecting meaning in RSVP at 13ms per picture." Attention, Perception, and Psychophysics, pp. 270-279. 2014, February.

Reich, J. "Practical Guidance from MOOC Research: Student Diversity." Retrieved from Ed Tech Researcher: http://www.edtechresearcher.com/2015/07/practical-guidance-from-mooc-research-student-diversity/. 2015, July.

Reicher, S. D., M. J. Platow, and S. A. Haslam. "The New

Psychology of Leadership." Scientific American. Retrieved November 17, 2017, from https://www.scientificamerican.com/article/the-new-psychology-of-leadership-2007-08/. 2007, August.

Siemens, G. "Connectivism: A Learning Theory for the Digital Age." Retrieved October 16, 2017, from http://www.elearnspace.org/Articles/connectivism.htm. 2004, December.

Suen, Hoi K. "Peer Assessment for Massive Open Online Courses (MOOCs)" 2014.

Suskie, Linda. Assessing Student Learning: A Common Sense Guide: San Francisco, CA, Jossey-Bass, 2009.

Topping, K.J. (2009) Peer Assessment. Theory into Practice, 48(1), 20-27.

Tuunila, R., and M. Pulkkinen. "Effect of Continuous assessment on learning outcomes on two chemical engineering courses: case study." European Journal of Engineering Education, 40, 671-682, from http://dx.doi.org/10.1080/03043797.2014.1001819. 2015, January.

Unknown. edX. "Introduction to Project Management." Retrieved September 18, 2017, from edX: https://www.edx.org/course/introduction-project-management-adelaidex-project101x-1

Wagner-Stafford, B., and J. Wagner-Stafford. Description of intellectual property. Rock Your Business: 26 Essential Lessons to Start, Run, and Grow Your New Business from the Ground Up: Toronto, Ingenium Books, 2017.

Walgreen, Bjarne. Refleksion Og Laering: Kompetenceudvikling I Arbejdslivet. Frederiksberg: Samfundslitteratur, 2013.

Bibliography

Wenger-Trayner, E. *Communities of Practice: Learning, Meaning and Identity.* Cambridge: Cambridge University Press, 1998.

Notes

1. Challenges of E-Learning

1. Peopleway

2. Putting the Digital in Learning

1. Manpower Group
2. Deloitte Millennial Survey
3. Wenger-Trayner, E.
4. Siemens, G.
5. Jasmini, V.
6. Ganapathy, S

3. A Model History

1. Handley, L
2. Margaryan, A., M. Bianco, and A. Littlejohn
3. Nielson, B

4. The Four Brain Quadrants

1. Kolb, D. A
2. Piaget, Jean
3. Wenger, Etienne
4. Illeris, Knud

5. Three Types of Learning

1. Piaget, Jean

6. Social Learning

1. Wenger, Etienne
2. Illeris, Knud

3. Glance, D. G., Forsey, M., & Riley, M

7. Experiential Learning

1. Mintzberg, Henry
2. Mintzberg, Henry
3. Walgreen, Bjarne

8. The 70/20/10 Model

1. Lombardo, Michael M., and Robert W. Eichinger

14. Creating Engaging Content

1. Merrill, M
2. Merrill, M.D.
3. Margaryan, A., M. Bianco, and A. Littlejohn
4. Margaryan, A., M. Bianco, and A. Littlejohn
5. Margaryan, A., M. Bianco, and A. Littlejohn
6. Margaryan, A., M. Bianco, and A. Littlejohn
7. Margaryan, A., M. Bianco, and A. Littlejoh

15. Ethos, Pathos, and Logos

1. Reicher, S. D., M. J. Platow, and S. A. Haslam
2. Aristotle, W. Rhys Roberts, Ingram Bywater, Friedrich Solmsen

19. Assessment Tools

1. edX. "Introduction to Project Management."
2. Topping, K.J.
3. Bruun, J., Reinecker, L.

20. Effective Assessment

1. Cranton, P.
2. Haladyna, T. M., & Rodriguez, M. C. (2013). Developing and Validating Test Items. Routledge.

27. Review the Five Steps

1. Parsons, A.

CPSIA information can be obtained
at www.ICGtesting.com
Printed in the USA
LVHW091225300720
661941LV00002B/226